PATRICK PUSEY

THE SECRET OF THE TALKING TREE

GRATITUDE - It is with a deep appreciation and gratitude feeling that I thank all my friends and family who contribute to bringing this book to fruition. I am so grateful to my beloved Cameran Frisbee for her kind support and advice.

Specials thanks to Emmanuel N'Gombet, David Mauntz, and Andy Bridge.

Blessings and love to you all.

First edition

ISBN: 978-2-9574879-8-1

Cover art by Andy Bridge
Editing by David Mauntz

This book was professionally typeset on Reedsy.
Find out more at reedsy.com

To Henri and Mauricette, for their hospitality.

"The way, the soul of the Earth,
is something you have to discover yourself..."

HENRI CRÂNE (1939 - 2014)

Contents

Foreword

By leaving the world that calls itself civilized, Henri has finally discovered freedom: here is an enigma subject to our curiosity... Together we can come to a firm and definitive understanding.

Live life! And in difficult moments, the three friends sing to give themselves courage. As nomads, they cross our world like crossing a bridge without even thinking of building a home on it. This sounds very strange without a little bit of spirituality, humanism, and ecology to allow us to reconcile.

Henri, Mauricette, and Maurice seek an ideal, overcome all kinds of obstacles; the final outcome of this story – happy and joyful – shows us that we can emerge victorious from the trials.

But above all do not forget that: "Science without conscience is only ruin of the soul" and all of society. "A word to the wise is enough!", says Henri with humor.

The future belongs to those who get up early. So why not you?

1

An Inner Revolt

The headwinds of fate nurtured their dreams: should they stay where they had always lived? Or should they give up work, family and nation for the colors of freedom and brotherhood? For the sake of hope...

In 1965, two French lads ushered in the New Year with a plan to escape their daily lives and explore what the world had to offer. Where would they go? They didn't know – but they wanted to leave this country which in their view had taken a wrong turn, a dangerous path: *the attraction of extreme materialism and mere individualism.* They had foreseen the dawn of a disaster whose insidious and devastating effects would gradually appear over the next 50 years...

Sad progress and happy tropics[1]*!*

At the time, Henri and Maurice were close friends and worked at Le Bourget airport near where they lived in Aubervilliers.

The company that employed them—The Flying Saucers—handled all aspects of food service and duty-free goods. Henri was assigned to the liquor and tobacco division working closely with customs. These two young people found it stimulating to be servicing international flights on the apron

---

[1] Play on words about the title of the book Tristes tropiques (1955) from Claude Lévi-Strauss, the 'father of modern anthropology'.

1

awaiting departure: BEA, TWA, SAS, KLM, Aeroflot, Lufthansa, Iberia and the UTA—Union of African Transport… The staff of foreign airline companies would approach them insistently in hushed tones, offering fresh baguettes in exchange for a few cartons of cigarettes or champagne at knock-off prices. A paltry affair for some, a treasure trove for others: just imagine enjoying Russian caviar…!

Watching the planes take off, they dreamed of being able to travel someday. But at the time, only the rich could afford to fly. When they looked at how much flights cost, they immediately realized – they had to find the cheapest way of doing it. Away from the bustle of the airport and the roar of engines, the two young men discussed how they would do it:

"Driving is better than flying."

"Flying's great if you're in a hurry."

"We have all the time in the world…."

"So yes—let's drive and see some countryside!"

"And for the price of a plane ticket, we can even pay for the food and gas we need to get there."

"By the way… just sitting here watching people set off makes me want to get going!" says Henri.

Henri and Maurice opted for the smallest Citroën they could find… They found a scrapped Post Office 2CV van, a real workhorse. Patiently and meticulously, they worked on it every evening as their means of escape.

The van repairs were going great. Always in a good mood and ready to joke with his mates, Henri, the mechanic of the duo overhauled the vehicle; he carefully checked connecting rods, pistons, rings, the crankshaft, cylinder head and the two air-cooled flat-piston cylinders that were the vehicle's powerplant. The steady chug of this engine would eventually drive them ever further south.

Maurice lent a hand and the two young men helped each other every evening on mechanical work. Little by little the "Deuche" became their new home. Expecting off road obstacles of every kind and not sure where they'd be going, they also focused on stiffening the suspension and they added four friction discs.[2] To be able to ford streams, they raised the ignition coil, attached it to the hood, and protected the distributor from water by wrapping it in plastic. Their slogan was: keep it simple!

They kept the van at 12 rue Paul Bert, parked right on the street. As for a garage or comfy shed, that was a luxury way beyond their very modest means. The parking spot in front of Henri's parents' home was big enough to let them work on their restoration among passers-by. Curious neighbors and onlookers occasionally asked how their preparations were going. The only thing left to do was find a roof rack at the Pantin flea market.

To outfit the interior of the car they recuperate secondhand thermoses and plastic plates coming from commercial airlines. They bounced ideas off each other. Maurice had the idea of strapping the big tap thermoses onto the panel walls for fresh water, hot tea or coffee. They also installed metal lockers for storage.

One fine day, they obtained permission to use the paint shop at the hangar. After finishing their day jobs around two o'clock in the morning, Henri and Maurice set to work with the paint gun to apply the final touches spraying the body black to cover the Post[3] van's corporate yellow.

Everything was going so well until the transfer of the headquarters of the airline food service hit them like a bolt of lightning. They were forced to follow their boss to the new airport at Orly located south of Paris. Since they aren't provided accommodation, it took three hours in city traffic to get to work and then three hours to get back. Their working day including commuting is now 15 hours.

The last straw was the strained human relations… The work was there, but their hearts were no longer in it. Organized as ethnically based corporations of Italian, Spanish or North African origin, their colleagues from other food service teams ostracized them. The cliques performed only routine tasks while dealings with aircraft and crews always depended on these two young new arrivals in a climate of constant urgency:

------

[2] Suspension solution before today's hydraulic shock absorbers.

[3] The French Post Office.

"We don't have time to breathe anymore!"

"They're taking advantage of us…"

"They couldn't possibly match the speed we work at…"

"This has really become impossible!"

So Henri and Maurice went to see their boss and resigned right then and there, face to face, saying without going into details that the situation wouldn't last long like this:

"If things stay as they are," said Henri, "you'll never be able to hold onto any French staff."

"There's no longer a remedy for this, goodbye," said Maurice turning his back.

The next day Maurice approached Henri, Paris newspaper in hand, shouting: "Hey Henri! Have you seen what's happening?"

The front page headlined a rare accident on the Orly airport ramp.

While maneuvering their tanker truck, foreign airport refueling crews had struck and severely damaged the wing of a superb DC-8[4].

---

[4] The Douglas DC-8 was the glamour intercontinental airliner of its day. This aircraft first flew on 30 May 1958 and was produced between 1958 until 1972 by the American Douglas Aircraft Compagny based in California.

2

The Crossroads

Anticipating the revolutionary events of 1968 in France, their life choice was not to conform but to travel abroad, a choice that would lead to a completely different life experience…

Necessity, Destiny and Providence had come together for a common resolution, but the dealer still held the dice and fate waited for him to roll them… Can they make the big decision? Will they decide to radically change their lifestyle overnight? Who would do so today? Around what values? Work to live or live to work? Their answer was "Simply to live!"—To live life…

One foggy night in Aubervilliers, something unusual happened: a Citroën sedan smoking and on fire appeared in front of 12 rue Paul Bert—a blatant suggestion to the police to investigate the mechanical servicing Henri was doing on his days off to make money on the side. Perhaps it was planted there by garages who were jealous of his roadside competition which they thought unfair.

His parents worried about all this and often, before dinner, his dad would talk about the subject:

"Why do you want to leave? You're nuts!"

"You have everything you need here: a job you like, a good salary… at just 26, you're earning twice as much as I do and you drive a DS!"

"But that's not it Dad. Don't you understand I'm suffocating here? I'm hungry for freedom! Don't you see things are on the wrong track... and with society as a whole?"

"No, I really don't. Where do you want to travel?"

"Africa."

"Okay, but where in Africa?"

"I don't know.... What I know is the direction. Due south."

"And Maurice, what does he think?"

"He agrees with me."

The dinner continued in silence his father having put an end to any further discussion.

At the end of the meal, as head of the table his father closed his folding knife. This ritual "clack" was the signal that family members could leave the table and the discussion immediately resumed:

"How will you survive with no money?"

"We'll find work, don't worry, you'll see, we're young!"

"My dear son, watch out, you may find nothing there..."

His mother was listening, gripped by fear as any mother would be, facing uncertainty over the future of her child. She kept her head down sewing, not joining in the conversation. Is this because it is men's business? More a matter of wisdom. Held back by a mother's tenderness, despite her heartfelt love for her son, she couldn't bring herself to sway him from what he had decided to do.

Patiently, Henri and Maurice had saved up three million francs, a large sum of money at the time. Henri tried to reassure the parents as best he could: "We've saved up a bit of money to cover living expenses while we're travelling; after that, we'll see..."

By sheer luck, Henri managed to acquire another used DS 19 from a garage owner in his neighborhood: "To get the car going, just slam the door! If you want it, it's yours..."

That's life. Happy to get rid of it, the dealer had been trying to repair this lemon for months with no luck until now. But he didn't know the young guy knew this car inside and out... It was now Henri's main vehicle, making the other tenants of his building and residents of this working-class suburb envious.

At the 26th Paris Air Show in Le Bourget, Henri having accepting a temporary mission, working alone on his shift finished his last day of work. At about one or two o'clock in the morning, he's driving home at 110 miles an hour when a Citroën 3CV crosses the grand boulevard! Driving on the Le Bourget bridge Henri clearly sees the green traffic light at the intersection just after the bridge but not the cars hidden by the upcurved deck. Crash! The speeding car hits the frail 3CV and knocks it across the ongoing lanes into some trees. Ejected from the DS, Henri rolls on the pavement:

"When will this be over?" he thinks to himself as he is rolling across the asphalt.

Finally sitting in the middle of the road he watches his DS go in reverse at a very high speed; horrified, he thinks: "It'll hit the bar and smash everyone inside, nothing can stop it… You poor souls!"

But miracle of miracles—a tree stops its crazy path right in front of a bistro! The DS has wrapped itself around one of the oak trees lining the avenue. The entire frame smashed into the tree. In the front passenger's seat nothing's left, no floor or roof; the seat's crushed. If anyone had been seated there at the moment of the impact, they would surely be dead.

Another car stops at the accident scene and its occupants approach Henri. Fortunately he's uninjured, not a scratch. As soon as he straightens up, he goes to help the driver in the 3CV. He soon sees the long blond hair of a young girl who's not responding. Her hands still gripping on the steering wheel, she is stunned by the violence of the smash. Henri struggles to wrench open the door and he asks her:

"Are you okay?"

"I'm okay…."

"Don't stay in the car, it may catch fire!"

He helps her get out of what's left of the vehicle. Fortunately, she's not injured and together they cross the road into the bistro. On entering Henri asks the owner to call the Aubervilliers police. The small group waits for the police to arrive to make an official statement. After recording what happened the police leave with the victims at the scene of the accident. Feeling abandoned the girl suddenly shows her dismay: "There are no taxis! I'm not going to stay here alone… What am I going to do?"

"I'll find someone to take you home," says the young Parisian.

In a few skillful maneuvers Henri frees the DS from the tree trunk. He puts it in gear, then reverse and turns the steering wheel left and right. Miraculously all its hydraulic systems are still working including steering as if nothing had happened! He goes home to his parents and tells them the happy news. He then goes to Maurice's place and rings the doorbell repeatedly waking up the parents who answer the door:

"Maurice, come down! Your friend Henri's here!"

"At this time of the night? What the heck is going on?"

"We just had an accident… Can you drive us to the Soissonnais?"

On the way back around ten o'clock in the morning with everything going well they come back through the Porte de Pantin and reach the suburb of Aubervilliers.

Henri drives the damaged DS to a garage and agrees with the tow truck to pick up the woman's wrecked 3CV: the two cars involved in the accident will be presented to insurance assessors. But to the great displeasure of the shop foreman who was hoping to make some money off of it, Henri offers his damaged car to an apprentice mechanic who had his eye on it. He never heard about the car again. All this is great for the apprentice, but bad luck for Henri because he now needs to cancel the sale of the DS the next day and give the money back to his pal Ranoud. Henri was counting on that money to top up his travel fund but events decided otherwise.…

When the big day arrives, Henri and Maurice follow through on their decision and say goodbye to their relatives and friends and leave them on very good terms: "We're going on a long trip, it may take years but we'll be back."

Two days later a friend of theirs named Mauricette joins them at the rendezvous point. They meet at *Café du Cimetière Parisien* in Aubervilliers situated very close to the L'Oréal perfume factory. Knowing very well that the young Parisian had difficulties being on time, Henri had given her an ultimatum: "If you're not at the rendezvous point at nine o'clock sharp, we leave anyway. So be on time for once or stay in Paris!"

She arrived at 8:45 a.m. sharp on June 21 ready to head off into the unknown with her friends.

3

Adapt or Disappear

The summer solstice gate opened and gazed upon this long-awaited day; on these remote, unknown but desired horizons.

A hunger for discovery—for knowledge—like the hunger that drives adventurers, great explorers, and men and women of good will. These are the following aspirations that drives this young trio along the beautiful ribbons of asphalt. They abandon the City of Light with its hectic life and its crowded suburbs to discover *the breath of nascent Africa.*

Negotiating a mass of vehicles heading against them into the capital, our heroes in the black 2CV swing onto national highway N10. The atmosphere onboard becomes cheerful and joyous: Versailles, Chartres, then Vendôme where the trio pass under a new highly symbolic arch, the Saint-Georges gate monument.

Their odometer counts off the kilometers. At 45 to 50 mph, the cities of Tours, Poitiers, Angoulême, Bordeaux and Bayonne roll past. Along the way faster vehicles overtake them. A few hours later, staying on course and maintaining their average speed, our three friends find themselves at the customs post in Saint-Jean-Pied-de-Port. They had crossed France in a single day!

A simple philosophy of travel and a shared quest animates them: the beauty of nature. That evening in Spain they set up camp near the border. They put up the two Canadian tents, make a campfire, eat on the go, and lie down to rest...

The enshrouding darkness of the night obscures the surrounding landscape; a torrent flows somewhere down the mountain. From cascade to cascade, the living water flows with a soothing rush. With the dawn emerges a harmony of light and sound from this small radiant corner; an indescribable feeling of tranquility and ephemeral peace.

They decide to stay put for now. Henri had already planned to take a shower under the spray of the cascade:

"I'm off to have a wash in the waterfall..."

"Don't even think about it, the water's way too cold," says Mauricette.

"I soaked my feet and that was enough for me," Maurice admits.

"Oh, how unadventurous! Suit yourselves, see you in a bit..."

A few days later they get back on the road in much the same way you get back on a horse after a fall; a little groggy, inwardly stunned but surely amazed by the changing scenery which remains calm and serene.

Paved roads turn into dirt and gravel tracks. In a hospitable countryside, they stock up with food mostly at markets in the main towns, especially cans and fruit. Passing through Madrid in the center of Spain, their wandering itinerary reaches the southern tip of the peninsula. The ride is actually quite comfortable thanks to the beefed-up suspension. Inside their trustworthy 2CV, they're pleased with their progress:

"We're making good time..."

"Yes, the track's not too bumpy. I'm managing to avoid the holes..."

"Look out! There's something white ahead..."

"What is it?"

Peering intently at the white thing in the road, Henri tries to work out what it is, without giving a thought to slowing down.

Suddenly, a big shock along with the noise of scraping metal – the trio are bounced around in the car against the doors, walls and ceiling. They finally realize: it's a rock, big enough to cause damage! They stop a bit further along the road. When they get out to check they find that one of the wheel rims is bent and unusable. Determined, the three young travelers enjoy taking action:

"Don't worry! We brought two spare wheels, two new tires, two new inner tubes, a pump, a jack, two tire irons, and the toolbox."

"So let's all get to work!"

Everyone pitches in. They get the wheel off and put a new one on…

"Now that we've stopped, everyone needs to pitch in!" notes Henri encouragingly, "Let's take advantage of this! And for lunch we can eat later; at noon, we don't have to stop to eat…"

"When the engine's running, it's time to drive!" he adds.

They load the damaged rim into the back of the van then leave. They can bang it back into shape with a hammer later…

By taking the Algeciras-Ceuta ferry via the Strait of Gibraltar they will be able to cross the Med in an hour and a half. At the port of Algeciras, the Aubervilliers trio set out to locate tickets for the next ferry. Near the docks, a Spanish character approaches them and offers them a deal:

"If you want, I can get you tickets."

He goes on to say, "Give me your passports and the ticket money and I'll take care of the boarding formalities for you; it may take several hours…"

It's risky, but the trio decide to trust him. They give him the money along with their three precious passports.

"In the meantime let's go get some coffee. I see tables in the shade of those trees…"

"Sure, no need to wait in line."

"We don't speak Spanish anyway!"

A few hours later their agent returns with the stamped passports and tickets. For a small fee he has done them a great service. Departure time comes: the 2CV rolls into the hold of the *Virgen de Africa* along with all the other vehicles and the passengers make their way to the upper deck. The trio is discreetly approached by one of the Spanish crew offering to exchange some French francs for Moroccan dirhams at a good rate. For a small fee, they accept even though it would have been less risky to do things with an official… Barely time for a drink, the ship's horn is already blasting signaling the passengers to go down to their vehicles. The three companions disembark in Ceuta, a Spanish enclave in Morocco; they declare their French currency when clearing customs.

The three companions radiate happiness. They're delighted, looking forward to entering Africa. Back in their 2CV they head for the Atlantic coast and reach Mohammedia Beach about 12 miles north of Casablanca. They set up camp on warm sometimes burning hot sand. A few days later, they find the comfort of an enclosed campground where trimmed hedges decorate the shaded pitches.

At sunrise, as they have done every morning, they get busy making breakfast. The water's boiling in the back of the van with the double doors open wide. Mauricette is supervising the preparations and watching over the gas stove. Meanwhile, as Henri and Maurice are peering at the vehicle's front suspension, they decide to push down on the body to check the shock absorbers which spills the pot of boiling water over onto Mauricette.

Shrieks of terror and shock!

Is their trip now in jeopardy or would they have to turn back? In this emergency, they didn't even have the time to ask themselves these questions.

Her entire lower leg is scalded to the bone which is now visible. Racing to help, Henri and Maurice immediately realize how seriously she's hurt and begin to treat her. By sheltering the wound with their hands, without touching, their magnetism causes the severe wound to start healing. Henri first, then Maurice takes over. These two men are equally capable of healing. Under Morocco's brilliant sun this urgent first aid takes less than five minutes. Was this more fear, than harm done? We can't say. Mauricette was certainly badly scalded, injured and shaken.

That same evening she decides to bathe in the sea and puts her misadventure behind her. Her suffering stops. Despite the exposure to salt water and sand on her wound, Henri and Maurice's magnetism form an invisible cataplasm. Since early childhood Henri had always wanted to, in his words, *learn to heal people* and since then he has developed extraordinary healing abilities.

4

Ahh, Africa!

The Atlas Mountains… A sleeping giant, the backbone of North Africa is made up of multiple ranges and its Western end drops abruptly into the Atlantic.

The route they had originally planned was to go along the coast through Mauritania. After talking with Moroccan locals, they realized the dangers involved:

"That's the route you're taking? People get robbed there all the time, it's not safe."

By mutual agreement, they adapt: this time, they head East following Morocco's Atlas Mountains to Algeria.

But under a soft azure sky, life's adversities can catch one in a surprising way, unexpected, almost disarmingly.

Halfway to Algeria, they stop for the night setting up camp near a small stream in a palace's park, south of Meknès. With its tall grass, Henri is sure the park meadow must be a waste land because it looks unmaintained. He is sure no one would mind them stopping there. A plausible thought perhaps, but no sooner do they arrive than an elegantly dressed official appears offering them little hospitality:

"Hello, do you know where you are?"

"No, not really."

"You can't stay here…"

Noticing the French license plate, he adds, "In France, would you pitch your tent on the Champs-Elysées?"

"No, of course not! Apologies, we'll move on…"

Realizing they won't be able to get anywhere with this guy, the trio leave the city and the Sultan's palace grounds and decide to camp on the side of the road. The next morning, they keep driving across the country.

In the High Atlas more than 12 thousand feet above sea level, the Citroën climbs a small dirt road strewn with gravel and stones. On this bright and sunny morning, high in the Atlas Mountains, the 2CV comes to a particularly steep portion on this road. "It's a hard climb! " says Henri behind the wheel.

Having stopped for a split second, without warning, the 2CV refuses to climb further. The driver keeps accelerating and the front wheels spin but nothing happens. Not wanting to stall the engine, he shouts out, "Maurice, get up on the hood!"

Maurice jumps out the door, rushes over to the front bumper and plants his one hundred and eighty pounds on it to add traction. But the thing still refuses to move:

"It's not working… Try getting back and push… You should have had more breakfast! You're not heavy enough."

Gallantly, Henri asks Mauricette to get out of the car and does a risky U-turn on this small road:

"Hey Henri, what are you doing?" says Mauricette, "Do you want to turn back?"

"Come on! Both of you get in the car!" shouts Henri, at his wits' end.

As Henri's backing up, they insist:

"What are you doing? Are you nuts?"

"If it's not able to move forwards; it won't be able to move backwards either!"

They don't understand what Henri is doing. He gets moving again by putting the car into reverse and driving up the hill backwards. He manages the hellish climb, along with a series of switchbacks, all the way to the summit. When he gets to the pass, he does another U-turn to face downhill. You could hear a pin drop, everyone holding their breath! Maurice and Mauricette are stunned and speechless. They can't believe what's happened…

"How the heck did you do that?" they say.

"Don't be dim, don't you know that the weight is in front with the engine and if you turn the car around it will be able to make it."

It will have better traction if you put the car's weight over the driving wheels. It's all about weight distribution.

"Driving isn't for idiots!" Henri adds provocatively. He enjoys seeing his companions react.

The wild mountain range is still reflected in the car's rear-view mirrors as the trio leave the foothills heading for the sandy plains. Tirelessly, the hours roll by and the trio eventually approach the Algerian border…

In the back of the van, Maurice sits like a pasha, leaning against the back doors. They're usually locked, but not this time… With Henri at the wheel and Mauricette sitting next to him on the bench seat, the 2CV suddenly hits a pothole and bounces violently. The back doors swing open and Maurice is thrown from the vehicle and he falls rolling in the sand.

Luckily the sand cushions his fall but Henri can't stop for him because he'd get stuck in the sand if he did. Instead he circles in a big loop to keep his momentum going to get his friend back. As he does so, he goes along with Mauricette to play a prank:

"Watch, I'll get him to run! And he hates running…"

As loud as he can, he shouts, "Run Maurice, run!"

Maurice runs to save his life. But Henri, a tease by nature, puts his foot down. He deliberately accelerates to outpace him, again and again. Maurice finally has enough and says, "I'm staying here! I'm not moving anywhere anymore!"

Henri slowly circles around to put him within reach and shouts, "Hurry up then!"

Maurice starts jogging, lunges at the car and pulls himself inside slamming the doors shut. In front Henri and Mauricette are laughing: "Did you enjoy your little adventure?"

Out of breath, a friendly retort from the back, "Just drive, you cunt!"

The atmosphere is often laid back and uneventful: they are just looking to spice up the monotony of the trip…

At first sight, crossing the Moroccan customs post seemed like a simple formality, but as they are showing their passports and getting them stamped the officials become bossy:

"Don't stray off the road before you get to the next village if you want to stay alive."

"You'll be driving through a minefield!"

So the 2CV takes the narrow track and Henri driving scrupulously respects the markers by not straying past them under any circumstances: too much to the left means certain death; too far to the right, ditto. On all sides the burned-out shells of cars and trucks have been blown up indiscriminately. The risks are obvious. On the bench the three companions remain calm. They put their lives in the benevolent hands of providence.

Risking his life in the mine field, Henri has a flashback from his early childhood. In his heart of hearts he holds a secret memory… At the age of six or seven, this child from Aubervilliers had the good fortune of meeting a Talking Tree in the East of France. This Tree, located at an isolated quarry, left such an impression on him that he has become driven to keep unraveling this mystery wherever it may take him in the world:

"Hey, I can't be the only one on the planet to have experienced this. Surely other people have too! But where are they?" He can't find anyone in France to explain this reality, so his only option is to go abroad.

Henri is snapped out of his flashback. Suddenly, to their astonishment a fork in the road appears!

Fortunately, there is a man nearby and the friends ask him which road to take. He gestures briefly to the right but Henri doesn't want to rely on a stranger's opinion: three lives depend on it. He didn't survive the Algerian campaign as a radio operator and road clearer to now jump on a mine and die during peacetime.

The trio decides to turn around and ask again at the Moroccan border. Watching them through binoculars, apparently unhappy to see them return, the chief customs officer is openly hostile:

"Why are you back?" he says brusquely… Suspicious, he adds, "Why were you talking to that man?"

The tension ratchets up a notch. Henri and Maurice reply:

"Why didn't you tell us about the fork in the road?"

"Which way should we go?"

"Right or left?"

"Right!" he snaps.

The three friends leave as they came, get in the car, turn right and finally arrive at Colomb-Béchar safe and sound. At the Algerian customs post the formalities go without a hitch…

5

The life school

In an isolated and deserted landscape, positioned two or three yards from the house entrance, a well emits an unpleasant smell. Grimacing, Maurice shows his disgust…

Nonetheless, his two friends ask the residents if they can draw some water. Helpful hands greet them and give them a bucket of water that the three travelers pour into their containers. In a low voice, Maurice mumbles, "You're disgusting to take this. I won't drink this water!"

Normally the brackish water from sub-Saharan resources doesn't smell. Perhaps the inhabitants of the desert were using the well to keep meat cool…

In his friendliest voice Henri advises his neophyte friend, "France is behind us, Maurice. We have a well for once, take some water and drink. Everyone else is drinking, so why can't you?"

An hour later under a burning sun Maurice asks:

"Hey Henri, give me a slug of your water…"

"Well… No! You said you wouldn't drink it but now you want a glass of my rotten water! It's my rotten water… and now you want me to give you a glass of water?"

"Come on! Don't fuck with me dickhead!" sighs Maurice. Henri pours him a drink and looks at his friend. "And he's loving this water, believe me!" he murmurs to Mauricette.

You have to adapt to the climate, and then to everything else too. From one day to the next, while crossing the Sahara, they're always on the lookout for water to replenish their vital reserves.

In a parched meadow, consisting of a bit of grass and a few trees, they see a herd of donkeys near a well. The 2CV stops and the three friends get out of the car and approach the brackish water hole. In this climate, fresh water like in France doesn't exist. Here, the water is slightly salty.

"Let's get some water," says Maurice who is about to grab the knob of an old wheel to drive the bucket chain. "Wait a minute!" warns Henri who, just back from the war in Algeria, wants to be cautious. He adds, "Let's see if the well is poisoned… First draw some water for the animals, we'll see if it's safe to drink."

At two or three o'clock in the afternoon, the animals must be thirsty… Maurice pulls up some water that flows into a kind of drinking trough. Under the searing sun, one has to work at the right pace so it doesn't become too frustrating. Too slowly and the buckets don't have time to fill up. Too fast and you deplete the well. Doing daily chores like these, Africans sing to forget the heat and fatigue. Henri sings:

♪ ♪ Pompons, pompons la merde, pompons-la gaiement, ♫

♫ Tous ceux qui me regardent, je les emmerde. ♪

♪ Pompons, pompons la merde, pompons-la gaiement, ♫

♫ Tous ceux qui me regardent, je leur mets le pied, le nez dedans. ♪ ♪

Maurice toils, wondering how long he should operate this big bucket chain: "As long as it takes to fill the bowl!" chime Mauricette and Henri, laughing…

"I'm the one pumping and you two are only good for laughing!" complains Maurice.

When the donkeys at the other end of the field hear the familiar sound of the bucket chain they all rush in braying. The poor beasts are thirsty: they quench their thirst for a moment then resume their search for food.

"Now you can draw some water to fill our jerry cans," says Henri, serious again.

Some time later, along the edge of the track, they meet a group of British. Henri remembers seeing this vehicle in Spain, then again in Morocco. It's a small tarp-covered Land Rover army style truck with right-hand drive. It is stopped halfway along a bend in the road, not the safest of places to stop to get acquainted. Six young men obviously very English climb out. Only one of them speaks good French, another one just sort-of. Our trio get along well with them as they're planning to cross the Sahara heading for Nigeria:

"So it's agreed, we'll drive together!" they conclude, and they all shake hands on it...

Under a blistering sun the crew of the Citroën set off toward the vast expanse of sand. The horizon reflects shimmering waves of heat that befuddle the senses... At the head of their strung-out convoy the French vehicle becomes in its pursuers' eyes a vague vaporous glow of a scout. Mystical landscape, arid land, inhabited solitude, land of improbable encounters, land of legends...

The trio drive ahead of the British crew. Approaching a wadi[5] the 2CV dives into the dry bed. Was it due to lack of experience that they didn't avoid the obstacle? Perhaps. Maurice drives like he would on French roads, taking his time to shift through the gears. Before they finished crossing, they remark that the huge wheels of a big truck had plowed up the riverbed and the ruts are too deep for the ground clearance of a 2CV. The car comes to an abrupt halt.

Henri says, "Go, go, go... put your foot down!" But in this fine sand, nothing works. Using their hands, with no shovels or traction mats, they dig painfully under the scorching hot sun—*over 120°F*. Half an hour later, arriving at the top of the bank, the Land Rover's crew join them and pass them a winch cable. They carefully draw up the slack on the line and after a toot on the horn, engines running, the two vehicles get going. They proceed in low gear thanks to the Land Rover[6] truck's four-wheel drive. Together, they finally reach a stretch of hard-packed sand.

---

[5] A wadi is a stream bed usually dry in regions of northern Africa. It often forms an oasis in a valley.

[6] Land Rover vehicles originate from Solihull, a West Midlands town in England (U.K.). The Solihull plant remains famous as the development site of the first Land Rover four-wheel drive vehicles in late 1947 and 1948. The Land Rover was intended to be an agricultural vehicle inspired by the wartime Willys Jeep.

Seemingly unimportant details become suddenly useful. Maurice learns to distinguish the softness of the sand by its color: "You have to pay attention to the colors!" he says, "With white sand, very white, there is a strong risk of sinking in. We're better off driving where it's stony, it's bumpy but we won't get stuck."

Exhausted, they've learned their lesson. "That's enough," they say to each other, "We're not doing that again!"

Hour after hour passes… Far in the distance, the Land Rover can be seen leading the convoy. Suddenly, without warning, the English stop and hop out of the truck. They set up a table, a few chairs, and some cups. Moments later, catching up, the trio stop and ask, "What's the matter? Have you broken down?"

Taking all the time in the world to enjoy their precious beverage, relaxing ostentatiously in their chairs, the six Englishmen reply drily, "No, it's time for tea!"

6

Adrar, oasis: light source

Bordering 300 miles of dunes, south-east of Colomb-Béchar, the town of Adrar is home to sparkling jewels of water.

You can tell there's water by the abundant vegetation. The oasis forms an experimental garden where brackish water is drawn from the ground by electric pumps. And for good reason: the town is big enough to have its own power plant. Through reservoirs and canals groundwater is distributed via an irrigation system that is used to supply homes, crops and plantations. Adrar marks a stage: the last haven of the civilized world after the semi-desert track; gateway to the sands of the Sahara.

The vehicles stop: they make a camp near the coolness of a pond where the trio set up their Canadian tents…

One morning, the trio decide to go for a swim in one of the large ponds:

"Hey Henri, come on! Let's go swimming!" says Mauricette.

"I'm just going to have a wash. Remember, I can't swim," says Henri.

They start happily horsing around, splashing each other. Then Maurice and Mauricette start to swim breaststroke.

"Come on, try to get me!" says Mauricette.

Henri considers trying to reach his friend at the other end of the pond, some tens of yards away. He takes a deep breath and dives in trying to achieve some forward locomotion. Holding his breath, he surprises himself and he flaps over to her.

"Hey, I can swim!" says Henri victoriously.

He realizes he can move in the water: first under, then on the surface. You just keep doing the same thing! He wins a victory over himself. That night, with two bursts of laughter, he confides to his friends:

"No one will ever believe I learned to swim in the Sahara," he chuckles.

Sharing the same feeling they all roar with laughter…

In these enchanting gardens the trio plan to stock up with food and water and check the vehicle's mechanics before the long 600-mile trip to Tessalit. They spend the next few days buying the provisions they need.

In the souk[7] they find two "gerbas": goatskin gourds that each hold about 8 gallons. What a surprise when they taste the water: it's undrinkable, putrid. These gerbas have probably been poorly prepared: normally goat skins are tanned before use, coated with "gatrane", a cade-oil-based preparation which keeps the water fresh and pleasant-tasting.

"I understand why desert nomads use only old gerbas…" Henri thinks.

Since they don't have bread, they decide to settle on crackers. So, they buy crackers! And thanks to the metal box, they're sure they must be well conserved… But they reek of diesel: perhaps having been contaminated in the cargo hold of a ship. The merchants probably dried out the consignment and put it up for sale. The trio would have had to open the packaging and taste the contents before paying to know - trust no one… Having discovering the scam, Maurice reveals his disappointment:

"I won't eat your rotten crackers!" he says.

But Henri brings them back to reality:

"When you're very hungry, you'll take a cracker… and eat it!"

They also buy two 5-gallon water cans. One of them turns out to be defective. It leaks! They'll have to do the entire trip with this jerrycan upside down:

"That way it won't leak and it'll be the first one we drink," Maurice adds.

In an unknown and different context, they would each grow individually thanks to meeting new people and encountering challenging situations. They

---

[7] Marketplace.

put this particular unfortunate experience behind them. They leave the jerrycan at the side of the road, happy to get rid of it, among piles of stone, scrap metal, and worn or shredded tires which serve as markers. In doing so they show the way to those who follow...

Behind them in the North-West are marked trails; and in the South-East, leaving Adrar behind, an ocean of sand blended between two colors: the azure blue of the sky and the ochre yellow of the desert; a relief of changing dunes as far as the eye can see and the beginning of navigation by dead reckoning with the help of a compass or the sun. Crossing countless lines of dunes gauging distances "as the crow flies" becomes meaningless given the ups and downs of the terrain, 100 miles ends up being closer to 150. When a vehicle burns 4 gallons of fuel per 100 miles, plan now for 8 gallons! That way, you'll be sure to get out of the Sahara...

That morning, along with the English crew, they leave Adrar, heading for the final military outpost lost in the sands. After a few hours by car, they find the soldiers there are strict and firm in their instructions. The head of the outpost tells each crew:

"You can't pass. For safety reasons you can only cross the Sahara in convoy. You can only pass if there are more than three vehicles. So, you'll have to wait... As long as it takes."

He also warns them, "You're determined to get through, that's fine. But there's no road, you make your own road. So if anything happens to you, no one will come looking for you! *You go at your own risk!*"

The English interpreter consults the trio about their confined situation; the next day is spent waiting in the heat and boredom.

Then renewed hope. A Peugeot 403 appears pulling a flatbed trailer with tarp hoops. On board, eight Algerians of all ages, children and adults, men and women. Our three friends suspect departure time's approaching...

But the Algerian group receive the same instructions:

"You can't pass. There aren't enough of you. Wait like the others... Wait for more vehicles to arrive."

The French, listening to the conversation, are beginning to find this rigidity stupid: the more days that pass, the closer their food and water supplies are to running out. And all this before departing! No way! Henri thinks for a moment: he comes up with a bright idea… He goes for the attack, asking Maurice and Mauricette to do the same and play along:

"Bring your plates, cutlery and bowls, because we're going to visit the head of this outpost right now!"

The French and the English reach an agreement. The small close-knit group of the three French and the six English present themselves in the refectory where about 15 men are gathered for dinner. They confront the highest-ranking officer:

"We have nothing to eat. Do you have anything to give us?"

"We'll be crossing other countries after Algeria!"

"Our food and water supplies have been carefully planned out, calculated for the duration of the trip."

"You're not letting us leave so you have to feed us!"

Reluctantly he gets them to sit at the table and has them served a thin soup. Actually it is more water than soup. The dinner goes well and before taking their leave, the guests thank their hosts for the food and return to their tents.

The next day the head guard comes to see the trio and says, "You can go, you'll be in convoy with the Land Rover and the Peugeot. Come to the office, we'll return your passports."

Their little ploy turned a perilous situation around to the benefit of all three groups of travelers. Henri, Mauricette and Maurice comply and quickly fold up their equipment.

Henri is very cheerful. He hums a happy tune from the 1900s sung by his father before the wars:[8]

♫Timélou, lamélou ♪ pan timéla ♫

♫ Paddy lamélou, concodou la Baya!

♫ ♪ Timélou, lamélou, pan timéla ♪

♫ Paddy lamélou, concodou la Baya! ♫

The modest Citroën van starts up and joins the Land Rover and the Peugeot

---

8   La Baya, *exotic song*, lyrics by Marcel Heurtebise, music by Henri Christiné, performed by numerous artists, and performed by Arletty in the 1930s.

at the head of the caravan. There, in this bluish landscape under a cloudless sky, traveled three valiant vessels.

And the Great South called them… To navigate, they follow a main point of reference: *the sun.*

The gateway to the Sahara opens up before Maurice and Mauricette's enchanted eyes. As for Henri, he had already experienced the Sahara during his military service in Algeria. They discover an almost endless expanse of desert and dunes with waves of blown sand stretching in all four directions.[9]

Every hour they adjust their course in relation to the sun. During the night, their caravan takes its bearings from the Milky Way and the stars… At dawn they check their course and Henri's Saharan experience does the rest.

With a hint of nostalgia, the three friends steal a last glance in their car mirror. Adrar takes on the distant reflections of a colorful and evanescent dream. They contemplate the memory of the now vanished oasis and shudder… "O Adrar, oasis… Where are you now?"

---

[9] The Sahara is a desert covering 3.5 million square miles, nearly the same size as the United States.

7

The Sahara, the world's largest desert

They come to the intersection of two tracks marking two Saharan routes frequented by camel caravans and intrepid travelers.

The plains route, which is the one our young friends had chosen, is like a string of beads linking Adrar, Reggane, Poste Weygand, Bidon Cinq and Tessalit. The mountain road, better known as the Hoggar Road passes through the community of Tamanrasset.[10]

At this crossroads, the convoy from Adrar encounters vehicles arriving in the opposite direction. Seeing them, they decide to stop: in this desert it's so rare to come across anyone… They greet each other and have a chat, swapping travel stories:

"Good morning!"

"Good morning! Where are you coming from?"

"We've come the mountain route. How's the track to Adrar?"

"It's ok… It's doable."

As they're talking, they realize they're dealing with teachers and professors who are returning to France on their summer holidays. For their first time driving through the Sahara, they have decided to make the trip by 4-wheel drive. In turn, the trio ask:

---

[10] Also known as Tamanghasset or (after 1981) Tamenghest, formerly Fort Laperrine, a city in southern Algeria, in the Ahaggar (Hoggar) Mountains.

"What about you? How's the road?"

"It's awful! 90 miles back, we came across four Land Rovers which have run out of gas, the families inside are all starving and thirsty, they had nothing left!"

"What happened?"

"They had started out as five Land Rovers, an English group forming a convoy to cross the Sahara. The Land Rover that was carrying all the spare fuel broke down… So they decided to abandon the car. As to be expected, when they ran out of fuel, they understood their mistake… Too late!"

As they recount their tale, the group of teachers tells them in no uncertain terms:

"Don't go there with your 2CV!"

"Even with our 4-wheel drive we had a hard time getting through."

"You'll never make it with your little car!"

As if words aren't enough, they get out of their vehicle and bang the hood of the 2CV:

"You won't make it!"

"We strongly advise you to turn around…"

"You have no idea what it's like!"

They also claim they've had a lot of things break: axles, drive shafts, leaf springs… "But if they've managed to get as far as this, why wouldn't I be able to get through?" thinks Henri, seething inside.

Deciding that they're just untrustworthy, he stops paying attention to their behavior. "Maurice, Mauricette, let's go! Enough time wasted! Let's go! Goodbye, have a good trip!" he bids them coldly.

And the 2CV hits the road again to Weygand Post… On soft sandy stretches the driver has to gear down and keep the engine revved up. In these desert conditions they find their suspicions were right—fuel consumption is twice as much as usual. They have to be careful not to fill the tanks and jerrycans to the brim since the fuel and fumes inside expand from the scorching heat! Henri tells his two friends, "When you're filling them leave an air gap at the top and be careful when you open them so we don't lose any fuel."

Through trial and error, they quickly come to the same conclusion themselves.

More experienced now, Maurice is now driving quickly and cleverly on the sand. Mauricette is sitting next to him and Henri is comfortable in the back, in "Maurice's ejectable seat" but this time leaning against the metal wall of the van. They've learned the lesson from their Moroccan misadventure.

In this overwhelming heat Maurice is becoming thirsty and asks for a glass of water. Mauricette is holding a bottle of water with an ill-fitting top in a bucket at her feet. The water has spilled into the bucket. Naturally, when she gives Maurice a drink, there's hardly anything left so she hands Henri the bottle to fill it up from the big thermos and says, "Maurice, stop. I'm going to empty my bucket."

But the driver has a better idea and he says, "No, no… Keep the water!"

They keep it going. One of them dips a cloth in the bucket. They serve Maurice his glass of water, which he savors in small sips. Meanwhile, Mauricette holds up the cloth and spreads it open in the air to dry it. When her arm gets tired, she scrunches it up again and wipes her face. Astonished, she says, "Say, it feels really good! Feel how cold it is!"

And she turns it into a little game, cooling Henri and Maurice down little by little. The two lads are immediately convinced. "How did you do that?" they ask.

They keep repeating the process, letting another water-soaked cloth flap in the wind. They notice that this little carousel game produces a cooling effect. "Go on, Mauricette!" they say, "Put the first cloth around the bottle and hold the other one back in the wind!"

They find through successive dips, that the water in the bucket becomes very iced and chills the whole bottle, making the water refreshingly drinkable. Under a burning sun and an ambient temperature of 120° F, for them it is a Eureka moment!

In the distance, there are two former military camps, abandoned by the foreign legion: Weygand Post and Bidon 5. Before reaching the first camp, the English wave at the Deuche to slow down:

"What is it?"

"We want to film the Land Rover while it's moving. Any chance of putting the cameraman in your 2CV?"

"Sure!" say the trio.

The English crew each have a speciality: a driver, a navigator, a cook, an interpreter, a treasurer and… a cameraman. They put the man and his camera in the back of the Citroën attached to the bumper with the two back doors wide open. The 2CV starts again, followed by the truck. The cameraman shoots as they pull ahead. Then Henri swings across to allow him to film the other side. He finally lets himself be overtaken to film the back of the English truck. Taking views from all angles, they ensure a beautiful result and it will be a happy souvenir of the trip.

A few moments later, they stop: the cameraman gets back in the Land Rover. Since he doesn't speak a word of French, they weren't able to talk to him. When they camp later, the interpreter comes to thank them and explains, "It's a TV movie and it'll be going to the BBC; you and your 2CV were filmed several times during the trip."

In the ruins of the military posts, the crews spend the night among the remains of stone walls and wooden barracks covered with corrugated iron. Like all travelers, Henri, Mauricette and Maurice write their names and the date they passed by on the wooden supports of the barracks…

Under a harsh sun, the Land Rover's 6-cylinder cast iron block tends to overheat. So, at Bidon Cinq the decision is made jointly to drive at night; the crossing of the Sahara will continue under the brightness of the celestial vault with the help of headlights. Under the soft, pleasant reflections of the moon, the cool night air will be equally soothing on the engines. That night, Maurice is driving the 2CV through the sand dunes with his two passengers half asleep. Suddenly, he exclaims:

"Hey Henri, wake up!"

"Oh, let me sleep. Just drive, don't bother me…"

"But look! In the headlights, can't you see the tracks of three vehicles?"

Slowly taking his time to wake up and open his eyes, Henri confirms Maurice's fears:

"They look like our tracks! Stop for a moment in the little car's tracks…

"These tire marks in the sand are exactly the same as ours!"

They get back in the car, wasting no time:

"We've done at least three laps in the dunes!"

"Quick! We have to catch up with the English!"

Finally reaching the English vehicle, they force them to stop. To convince them, they point to the tracks left by the Land Rover, shouting, "We're going around in circles! We have to catch up to the Algerians!"

Being faster than the trio, the English reach the Algerians first and stop them. With most of the passengers asleep, the driver and the only other man awake say, "No, no! This is the right way; we need to continue straight ahead!" The English show them the fresh tracks. Sheepish, the two Algerians recognize their Peugeot's tire marks.

Driving around in circles, they would have run out of fuel very close to the border.

At night, in the desert, the convoy needs everyone to stay vigilant. One has to remain alert and awake, because every person can make the difference. During the day, it's so hot it makes it impossible to stop and sleep...

It's morning, eight o'clock. The English navigator, shaken awake, takes out the compass and map to work out where they are. To verify, they can finally use the sunrise as a guide. The convoy sets off again for the Algeria-Mali border and the three vehicles finally leave the tire marks behind them.

At the end of the convoy, Henri has taken over the wheel. The three vehicles are moving at high speed, close together. Suddenly, hitting something in the sand, a child tumbles from the back of the crowded Peugeot. He falls heavily onto the stones; unresponsive, perhaps knocked out... Henri manages to brake just in time. In the heat of the moment, he reacts by standing on the brake as hard as he can; no time to think of turning the steering wheel. The 2CV stops abruptly: the child lies just inches from their bumper.

He honks a few times to warn the English and Algerians: "Stop! Stop! Stop!"

The English haven't noticed a thing and the Algerians don't hear him: Are all the passengers asleep?

The child is bleeding profusely. Grabbing coagulants from the first aid kit, the trio take an hour and a half to swab his wounds and bandage them. They administer an oral coagulant to provoke a reaction.

They save his life.

They put him in the 2CV and start driving again. In Tessalit, as soon as they arrive, they're reproached by the Mali customs officer, "The other vehicles arrived two hours ago! Why are you so far behind?"

"We have an injured child. He fell out of the car in front," they reply calmly.

Without further delay, they go straight to the local hospital. They hand the rescued child over to the authorities who take over from there. At the customs post, the Algerian group doesn't even notice that one of their children is missing. In fact, he had remained unnoticed…

8

Return to civilization

I n the town of Tessalit, situated in the Adrar of Ifoghas region, the French trio rush headlong to an establishment reputed to be the international airport's grand hotel, called *Hôtel de France*.

They dream of taking a good shower, having not washed for the seven days it took to cross the Sahara.

In the lobby, Henri notices there aren't any guests. "There's no one here…" he murmurs in Mauricette's ear.

Inside the building, they head for the bar and order a refreshing house drink. The bartender serves them a fruit juice without ice shavings or ice cubes. And for good reason: there's no water!

The Aubervilliers trio enjoy their first-ever taste of mango juice and discover the delicious pulp of this exotic fruit.

In the evening at the restaurant, efficient staff serve them a hearty meal at their solitary table, but the tasty dinner comes with only one glass of water per guest:

"Could we have a carafe of water, please?"

"That's not possible sir, but if you wish, you can have wine…"

"No thanks."

Between themselves, the three friends comment on the service:

"They will sell you food for next to nothing, but a glass of water for the price of the meal!"

"But you can have all the wine you want."

"We don't drink wine."

"Water's like gold here."

"Even if we offered gold, we probably couldn't have water!"

During dinner, the conversation quickly turns to the facilities offered by the hotel:

"We asked about a shower when we came in…."

"The receptionist didn't reply… Shower time was over!"

"I learned from a floor attendant that there's water only once a day and only for ten minutes."

"You have to be fast to take a shower here!"

The building has real showers with running water. But after shower time, the rest of the day, there's no water anywhere because it's turned off.

The next day, everyone's ready at the scheduled time under the shower head, faucets open, waiting for the water to flow. Little things like these help Mauricette and Maurice to better understand the discipline imposed on them when crossing the Sahara. Normally, the daily ration for one person is three liters of water. But Henri, based on his experience, reduced it to one liter of water per person per day, plus a large salt pill each morning.

The next day, when they leave the hotel, the three friends are laughing.

"This is the only time we've deliberately gone to a hotel to take a shower… and by a stroke of bad luck, we missed the shower!" they say.

They now hit the road to Gao. It alternates between sand and orange clay[11] roads, but the Deuche behaves perfectly. They arrive safely at the city outskirts and go to the souk to get supplies.

This Tuareg[12] city borders the Niger river, the main artery of West Africa.

Imagine a big city, where livestock herds led by their guardians swim across or ford the river. Imagine fishing boats on the river and a market where all

---

[11] Laterite is a reddish clayey material, hard when dry, forming a topsoil in some tropical or subtropical regions and sometimes used for building.

[12] Berber people of the western and central Sahara, living mainly in Algeria, Mali, Niger, and western Libya, traditionally as nomadic pastoralists.

kinds of food are displayed, a jumble of dates, figs, citrus fruits, fish and meat.

Imagine...

Amidst all this joyful chaos they see a powerfully built man, certainly a local Mali, hawking potatoes in 3-pound bags. The trio are surprised to find a product of the earth that their stomachs are familiar with:

"Look! Potatoes!"

"How much for one bag?"

The seller demands an exorbitant price. They discuss, and decline what they consider an extortionate offer. They go on their way to other stalls; while doing their shopping, they manage to tour the entire market. The man sees them again, hawking his potatoes.

They answer firmly, "No, we haven't changed our minds!"

A few moments later, they get back in the car. As Maurice is driving in traffic, he stops at an intersection, then pulls off at this signal. Henri is sitting in the back of the 2CV when he suddenly sees the big potato hawker open one of their van doors and throw his bag of potatoes inside. Surprised by this intrusion, Henri reacts promptly:

"Go Maurice! Drive! Drive!"

"What is it?"

"Don't worry about that! Put your foot down! Accelerate!"

They pull away from the wild-eyed guy who is running like a lunatic after the 2CV. In epic fashion they end up with a "gift", as it were, a bag of potatoes...

.

A few miles later, they see herds grazing on the bank of the river. A cowherd, who has prepared a young animal, is selling freshly slaughtered meat to passers-by. Mauricette jumps with joy and says, "Great! Let's buy a nice steak!"

The man hacks off the ordered amount with a machete, right there and then: the machete serves as a tool for work and survival, it protects... It does everything! That's life!

In an African village, everything happens as if children came into the world with a machete in their hands. This often brings a smile to travelers' faces, surprised to see a five-year-old kid carrying a machete as big as himself, trailing it in his little hand.

Henri, Mauricette and Maurice buy three beautiful pieces of rare meat, which they will eat with some of the potatoes that were pushed into the car. The seller uses a pair of balance scales to work out the price. The meat costs next to nothing: they'd have bought more, but how would they keep it fresh? For their meal, the slices of beef are grilled in olive oil, in a frying pan. The accompaniment is cooked in water on a small camping stove fed by a gas bottle. Tender, delicious meat! What a feast! What a contrast! Since they started their journey, they've only eaten canned goods. It's the only time in their entire trip that they've had a nice rib steak!

"Even at the hotel, they couldn't spoil us this much!" they say, in a great mood.

At nightfall, on its way to Nigeria, the English Land Rover stops near the trio's camp. The three go to meet them:

"What are you doing here?" they ask.

"The same thing you're doing…"

"We're going to spend the night here."

The interpreter approaches and tells them, "This is the last time we travel together… We are going our separate ways!"

Taken aback by surprise, the French trio return to their camp without exchanging a word. They don't understand why the English are so blunt with them. The next morning, our three friends are the first to wake up, have breakfast and hit the road. After a furtive glance, they abandon the English crew to their wishes. Thus, turns the wheel of Destiny…

They come across a very difficult stretch of land full of sand and thorns. The shrubs have thorns topped with long spines – about 4 inches long. These come loose, fall and are littered throughout the soft sand. Once in this trap, the 2CV keeps getting flat tires. From sunrise to sunset, Henri and Maurice take turns dismantling the wheels. They patch the inner tubes, put the tires back on and inflate them with a manual pump. While one is driving, the other prepares the next tire as a replacement in the back of the van with Mauricette's help.

With their vehicle being light, they don't sink much into the soft sand but they get lots of punctures: today, they've had 20 flat tires. It takes them all day to drive 18 miles. Tired and disheartened, they decide:

"Forget about eating tonight… Let's just sleep."

"Yes, let's just stop and see what happens tomorrow."

Next morning, they're back on the road. As the new day dawns, everything seems to be going well. Then around noon: pow! Another puncture! They stop at the side of the road. As they're working on the flat tire, they hear the rolling sound of thunder gradually approaching. As they listen, it sounds increasingly like a load of scrap metal rattling. Henri stops working and asks Maurice, "Hear that noise? What the hell is that?"

"Oh, that's nothing! I bet it's the Land Rover!" he answers.

A few moments later, they watch the cabover truck go by. Hurtling at full speed along the corrugated track, it soon disappears in a cloud of red dust.

God willing, they'll never see each other again. Abandoned at the side of the road, broken down, they've run out of patches not far from an African hut village. Fortunately, an African appears and the two young men jump at the opportunity:

"Ask him if he has any patches."

"You never know."

They talk for a while and then swap a liter of brake fluid for two precious patches. Everyone's happy with their barter. The trio can fix two wheels and leave the beautiful spiny shrubs, once and for all.

Next morning, the 2CV follows the line of the river and crosses the Mali border. At the entrance to Niger, it is stopped by customs officials. While one of them checks passports, the other talks to the three travelers:

"Anything to declare?"

"A little money: five hundred francs, that's all."

Looking at the 2CV's antenna, he adds:

"Do you have a radio?"

"No, we don't."

"But you have an antenna."

"Yes, but we don't have a radio."

"If you have an antenna, you must have a radio."

Maurice, exasperated, replies, "Have a look yourself, go on and search." The zealous customs officer starts to haul everything out of the car: the gun and luggage go on the ground. All of a sudden, he points to the big airline thermos and asks, "And this! What's this?"

Henri turns the spigot and out runs water, then coffee, tea… and replies:

"Want some?"

"No!"

The customs official searches the car for an hour. He takes everything out and then puts it all back. Tetchy that he hasn't found a radio, he hands the trio back their checked passports. A few miles later after leaving customs, the three friends from Aubervilliers stop the Deuche.

From the big water thermos, they remove a plastic pouch weighted with a small stone and out comes a wet wad of bills. During this impromptu break, at noon, they hang the wet bills one by one on a string stretched between the roof rack and a tree. Held by clothespins, the bank notes dry in the wind.

9

Great African hospitality

The adventurers head for the capital of Niger. Near Niamey, they set up camp on a hill a mere stone's throw from the big river when suddenly a car approaches them. It stops right by them and a European woman gets out. They quickly size her up: "This isn't someone from the outback."

The woman asks them, "Hello… What are you doing here?"

"Hi! We've set up camp for the night. See for yourself… Our tents are up," they answer.

"You are the first-ever campers in Niamey!" she says, "We've never seen any around here before. But you shouldn't stay here! Come to my house. You can stay at the house."

They barely have time to fold up their gear when her husband arrives by truck and offers to guide them. About a mile later, they approach a home built in typical Nigerian style: five round huts, arranged around a large central courtyard. Each hut has a purpose: a kitchen, a lounge, a dining room, a bathroom and a bedroom. The host and hostess promptly announce:

"We are going away for the evening; we've been invited to diner."

"Feel free to use the lounge, you can stay there."

"Our house is open… Nothing's locked. If you get hungry, just help yourselves. You'll find everything you need in the fridge."

At first the three friends feel slightly bothered by such hospitality but they're quick to adapt.

That's the way of life here.

The next morning, when the owners return, the trio get to know this young French couple better. They are both passionate about photography and hunting. The man earns his living catching birds and other animals to sell to circuses and zoos in France. Even antelopes and giraffes… His wife helps him capture birds with brightly colored plumage for people in Europe. She does so by setting small traps using seeds as bait. On top of that, she is also a press correspondent for Paris-Match: "I occasionally send articles," she says.

While talking, the couple take them on a tour of their animal park where the different species are gathered. Several Nigerians are employed to fish the river, feed the captive animals, or serve as park rangers. The three friends then have the chance to watch some impressively large vultures. They throw fish to the birds of prey in flight, who use their sharp beaks to grab them. As tall as a man, these raptors aren't as evil as they look… provided they're fed. They only go after cadavers. These scavengers aren't harmful; they are necessary for the life of the country. The trio is also impressed to see Niger crocodiles…

After the tour, the five French return to the huts. In the lounge, among magazines and books, Henri sees a book that is familiar to him: *The Morning of the Magicians*[13]. The subtitle reads "Introduction to Fantastic Realism." The text is described as "a story, sometimes mythical and sometimes accurate, of a first journey into areas of knowledge that have barely been explored."

The Parisian starts to relax. He understands that he has just met young people who are open minded. Henri is happy to be able to converse and share ideas about this recent book:

"This groundbreaking work talks about an unspoken way of being open to life, passed across generations in silence…"

"It echoes a very current philosophical theme at the dawn of the nuclear age…"

---

[13] Le matin des magiciens, Louis Pauwels et Jacques Bergier, éditions Gallimard, 1960.

"Science without conscience is only the ruin of the soul…"

"Indeed, the Consciousness of God inside and outside in intimacy with the consciousness of the awake man… and of the awake woman."

"To shed light on the subject, both coauthors use alchemy as an example."

"And it illustrates the transmutation of the alchemist himself by the union of microcosm and macrocosm."

"To be or not to be? Whoever can ask themselves that question, does. At least, provided that Man—from his earliest years—is not diverted from the Way, Truth and Life!"

"Above all, freedom of thought must not be taken away! Otherwise, there would be nothing!"

During these few days, Henri, Mauricette and Maurice greatly appreciate the hospitality of their new friends. In the shade of a hut, they do a quick overhaul of the 2CV. When it's time to leave this expatriate couple, they part affectionately and then head for Konni, a town 180 miles east of Niamey.

Frequently, along the road, they see young Nigerians signaling, raising their arms with two clenched fists as the 2CV goes by. One clenched fist is fine… but two clenched fists are too much for Maurice. "Henri, stop the car! They want to beat the shit out of us!" he says nervously.

Henri and Mauricette reply, "You're wrong, they're just saying hello. Look at them, they're smiling, beaming—look how happy they are to see us!"

This is surely their way of greeting us, they conclude with a smile.

Putting this behind them, the three friends meet the next day a young European on horseback. "Hi, how's it going?" he says, a little worried. "We're good thanks!" they answer, showing they're friendly.

He has never seen a Paris-registered 2CV around these parts. For him, it's so cool! By his body language and way of speaking, they immediately recognize a Frenchman. They learn that his parents are teachers in a Nigerian school. They ask him:

"Where are you going?"

"I'm going home…. I live down the road."

"Hey, you have a fabulous horse!"

Maurice, a keen rider, starts talking with the teenager about horses. In this sandy landscape, there's nothing wrong with going for a ride pretending you're in the wide-open spaces of the American West… In the meantime, Henri unhooks the two gerbas strapped to the side of the van; he intends to abandon them here to lighten the vehicle. But he thinks, "Would you like some gerbas?"

"Sure!" answers the enthusiastic teen.

Henri pours the water from the gerbas out onto the sand. They don't need it anymore because they now get their water from the rivers. Maurice hands the straps of the gerbas to the young rider who will now go home with two very singular gifts. The 2CV continues towards the town of Maradi. The trio go to the police station, where they clear Nigerian customs.

That same day—*August 4*, they enter Nigeria…

10

Prisoners of the English

The Nigerian embassy in Niamey issued them a five-day transit visa to reach the Cameroon border crossing.

As soon as they enter the country, they feel hostility.

They stop at customs and show their visas; but the British customs officials want to inspect the van. During the search, one of them starts shouting… Of course, Henri, Mauricette and Maurice don't understand a word! The Anglo-Nigerians have found a 22-caliber rifle belonging to Maurice.

Taking advantage of the confusion, Henri agrees with his friend:

"The rifle's not doing us any good, let's get rid of it."

"Sure!"

Putting words into action, Henri picks up the offending gun and throws it across the border into the French zone:

"Leave it there, say nothing more."

But the British aren't deaf:

"No! No! No!"

The case is not closed, the rifle is retrieved and confiscated. They then bring the trio into the customs house to count the ammunition. Maurice sits in front of the Chief Customs Officer and, with a great show of nonchalance, he takes the ammunition out of the boxes and tips them into a bowl in front of him one by one, counting out loud:

"One…, two…, three…, four…, five…"

The pile gets higher and bigger. Suddenly, the chief customs officer leaps from his seat like a deranged puppet: "Stop it! Stop it! Stop it!"

Surprised, Henri asks, "What have you done? Did you kick him?"

"No, no idea what's wrong with him," replies Maurice.

The Customs Chief picks up the ammunition to count himself. Certainly, he's thinking, "These French are stupid; you can never order them around!"

He finally has their passports stamped, but makes them go to Kano, a city 120 miles away, to register the rifle. And since they're not allowed to own a firearm, he assigns them an escort. In the 2CV, they are now escorted by one of his customs staff.

At lunchtime, they see the poor Nigerian doesn't even have any food. "Come and eat with us!" they say, inviting him to share food and drink.

When they show up at the Kano customs post, the officials seize their passports, rifle and ammunition. They then drop them off at the appropriately named *Hôtel de France* at the trio's expense.

The next day, they find out that no progress have been made, everything's on hold; in bad French, they hear, "We haven't found an interpreter."

With numerous mimics and gestures, the customs staff explain that they will have to go back to the hotel and wait.

On the third day, it's the same thing all over again at the counter. But this time Henri reacts immediately circling his finger at his temple, he says:

"Hey, what's wrong with you? This has gone on long enough!"

"What about food?" rubbing his thumb and forefinger at his mouth.

"What about money?" rubbing his outstretched thumb and forefinger.

He uses universal sign language to respond to the British officials. When the customs officials go into a big huddle, Henri loudly demands to be put in touch with the French embassy in Nigeria… This will have unpleasant consequences. So, the customs officials decide to return their passports, rifle and ammunition. They wave them on: "Fair sailing! Best of luck!"

Egoistically, Maurice reacts, "They're not going to send me away that easily!"

On the contrary, with no further convincing, Henri seizes the opportunity and says to Mauricette and Maurice, "No need to discuss! Come on, let's go! Get in the 2CV! If they're letting us go, let's go quickly!"

At last they leave. The three friends pay the hotel for their three days and head off on the road to Bauchi… Their visas expire in two days.

In those days, Nigeria was the only country in West Africa where people went naked: men, women and children. In villages and by the roadside, some wore just foliage secured by a piece of vine around the waist. It was the traditional Nigerian costume. In cities, the British dressed in colonial style: patent or white shoes, socks, Bermuda shorts, white shirt, epaulets and light hat. Shocked, the three French understood what the British contingent of their Saharan convoy may have wanted to hide from them…

After the city of Bauchi, they head east towards the village of Yola. In the middle of the forest, the small winding road leads to a bridge. The driver stops and the three friends go on foot to check if the bridge is strong enough to take them. After a few steps they can see the bottom of a precipice with a whitewater river 100 feet below them. When they start crossing, bits of wood fall off and crash to the bottom of the ravine…

The three friends are shocked:

"What the heck is this?"

"We have to drive over that?"

"There's nothing between the planks, you can see right to the bottom!"

The mechanic of the trio decides to take charge and says, "You two will cross on foot, be careful, watch where you put your feet! You'll be adding at least a 250-pound load as you cross together."

At the wheel of the 2CV, Henri approaches. Very slowly, he drives onto the half-rotten wooden bridge and says, "Above all be careful, guide me well! Watch my wheels, because it's really narrow!"

From the other end, Maurice focuses on Henri's driving, using hand signals to guide him: a bit to the right or a bit to the left. Henri follows his instructions to the tee. Some worm-eaten pieces come off and are swept away by the torrent. The Deuche does its best to cross the dilapidated bridge, but alas they come across another wooden bridge in the same condition. To cross the bridges, the driver has never sweated so much in his life!

At night with the thick forest enveloping them in darkness they sleep in the 2CV on an elephant trail. The next morning, waking up, Henri checks the oil level:

"Shit! The engine's out of oil and the oil can is empty. With all the problems involving the English, we forgot to buy oil." He comes up with the idea of topping it up with two cups of *vinaigrette sauce*. It's better than nothing.

When they arrive at Yola, they see a village with a massive mountain range behind it. Our three friends are taken aback:

"So, where is the road? Look… there isn't any although it's clearly marked on the map. There's not even a gas pump. This place is more deserted than the Sahara!"

Henri is convinced that he will soon find a way out of this dead end in Yola. It can't be any other way. His destiny is to understand how God comes to live in man and how man can get closer to God, his Creator, during his lifetime.

11

Lost in Nigeria

The trio learn that the road between Yola and Garoua—in Cameroon, has never been built… They can't go any further so they decide to turn off the engine and camp.

The next morning, the trio return to the vehicle. Henri turns the key repeatedly:

"What's happening to this bitch? It doesn't want to start anymore!"

The irony of it all: they've broken down in the jungle; caught in the bottom of a hollow! A dead end: Yola.

The mechanic mulls over in his head, "What's keeping the engine from running? Could be a seized connecting rod or valve…. we have to troubleshoot this."

Then he says to Maurice, "No one's about to come by to help us. Come on, let's get to work. Hand me the toolbox."

They remove the hood and the fenders, drop the fan and unhook the spark plug leads. While Maurice turns the starter, Henri watches how the two cylinders react: on the right side he hears a chug; on the left side nothing—it seems stuck. After some thought, he decides the left side is the culprit. They remove the head and then free the cylinder, no problem so far. The cylinder, piston and valves are okay. During this open-heart operation, they find that the crankpin has a seized rod that has become welded to the crankshaft: their patchwork solution wasn't enough… They decide to cut out the connecting rod. But how?

"Get me a hacksaw," says Henri.

"I've looked, there isn't one in the toolbox…"

"Seriously? We didn't bring a hacksaw with us? Shit!"

Henri is becoming increasingly loud.

"Figure it out! Find us a hacksaw…"

"What are we going to do now?" Maurice sighs.

Discouraged, the two friends sit in the 2CV to clear their heads. Time passes slowly. After ten minutes of dead silence, Mauricette is startled when she suddenly hears cries of joy. Maurice has found a piece of a hacksaw blade abandoned in an air vent of the 2CV:

"We can cut out the rod!"

"Come on, let's get back to work!"

To better hold the broken blade, they wrap the tip in a cloth. For more than an hour, they saw both ends of the rod to remove it. They hit the side with a hammer. It breaks, leaving the head attached to the crankpin.

Euphorically, they shout, "We did it!"

"Hey, let's have a drink! Good job!" adds Maurice.

Mauricette makes them coffee.

Not entirely sure, Maurice asks, "You're sure it's going to work?"

"Sure of nothing! But it has to work!" answers Henri.

The mechanic sees his friend troubled by doubt. He tries to boost his confidence, saying, "Give the starter a quick turn, you'll see."

Starter on, a cylinder moves and if proof be needed a splash of oil hits them in the face. That's a good sign! It's starting to look good… No time to waste, they start reassembling:

"Come on, give me the cylinder. I'm going to fit it! Not the piston, dummy! It's in your pocket, don't mess around! Now, the cylinder head… and the two pushrods, that too, hang onto them, I don't need them right now! For ignition, find me an old spark plug and a long lead."

Henri wraps the faulty cylinder with wire to keep the old spark plug in place. He dismantles the other spark plug and makes the connections. Then he triggers the starter. Maurice sees sparks: "Your old spark plug's working!

But it's sparking in the air…" In this way, they protect the ignition coil which can't burn up when balanced: a spark from each side. Henri and Maurice fit the spark plug of the right-hand cylinder and put the fan, the two fenders and the hood back into place. They start the engine. Its subtle chug becomes as loud as a farm tractor: "Pum, pum, pum, pum …"

It's running! And the engine's speeding up! Big smiles spread across the faces of the two French lads. Henri breaks into a victory song:

♪ Ti ploti – nestaqué ♪ nestaqué ♪

And nicolendo – and chila poulpa – and nicolendo

♪ Et chila poulpa – poulpaque ♪ poulpaque ♪

Lightly, gently, he jokes with Mauricette: "Whether you are ready or not, we're off…"

Noon arrives, before finally leaving, they hide in their tent so they can eat without making the impoverished kids of the village envious. The children will grab any cans left behind to turn them into toys…

That same evening, the three friends leave Yola. But after a mile on the road, the battery warning light comes on: the alternator's no longer working! They stop, lift the hood and notice that the long central bolt of the fan is missing: "Ah, more trouble! Where has the bolt gone!" The three friends decide to return to Yola on foot searching along the road for the long bolt with the light of a lamp. They return to the car and finally discover it by feeling around the inside of the rim of the hood. "There's your bolt!" says Maurice.

They head back to Bauchi and cross the two rickety bridges again. In Bauchi, they head for Dikoa in north-east Nigeria. Afterwards they branch off at Mubi to get to Garoua, Cameroon.

Along the way to their destination, they realize that the van struggles going up hills. They cope with this by downshifting. When the Citroën is in 1st gear, Henri moves aside and lets Mauricette slide in behind the wheel to accelerate so the boys can get out and push the van: "Push hard, you big dummy!", exchanging friendly jokes. All the hills require this method: the boys are pushed to the limits! At the top, Henri a bit breathless, slips back behind the wheel…

One morning, halfway between Bauchi and Dikoa, the Aubervilliers trio stop on the main road to have breakfast. Suddenly, they see a vehicle pop up. "Who is this guy?" they wonder, "Is he lost?"

The car slows down and stops beside them. They're French! The driver is showing his young wife Africa; it's her wedding present. Thanks to this excursion, she's starting to enjoy African life. During the conversation, the newlyweds announce that they are going to Yaoundé. Since the engine of the 2 CV obviously needs a new crankshaft, the young couple agree to give Henri a lift along with them while Maurice and Mauricette continue the journey to Garoua.

Arriving in the afternoon, he rushes to the Citroën garage while the newlyweds have lunch in a restaurant. On his return, Henri meets them at the restaurant and asks them if they can drop him off. Meanwhile, Mauricette and Maurice arrive in Garoua, designated as the rendezvous point. On the 700-mile long loop from Yola to Garoua, the 2CV makes it on a single cylinder without throwing an ounce of luggage overboard.

Henri doesn't get to the rendezvous point until the evening. The next morning, crankshaft in hand, he reunites with his two friends and he is surprised to see them already comfortably installed next to a garage:

"What are you doing here?"

"We got talking with a French guy, he's a mechanic, his wife's English... We found a place to stay and he is letting us repair the 2CV in his garage.

Once again, it would appear that Providence has saved them... Without realizing it, Mauricette, Maurice and Henri had crossed back into Nigeria without a *new visa!*

In the joy of the moment, they introduce Henri to the Franco-Nigerian. The next day, he invites them to the festivities given in honor of the authorities, "But you can't come dressed like that, guests dress smart!" he says. He lends the two young men each a suit with white shirt and tie. The sizes are wrong, they're dressed like penguins but it seems to suit the English hosts: "Don't worry, no one will notice a thing." More resourceful, Mauricette had the forethought to put an evening dress and pump shoes in her suitcase.

The next day, Henri decides to tackle the job of repairing the Deuche. But the Nigerian garage owner faces an unforeseen problem. "I have the

President's limousine in the workshop… The brakes are overheating… My staff don't have a clue about American cars…. Could you take a look?" he says to Henri and Maurice.

Henri starts by loosening the brakes: they're too tight, the linings would have overheated and could have caught fire. Then, with a jet of compressed air he clears out the dust. Finally, he readjusts the brakes and tries out the limousine in front of the boss and the driver. Everything works fine.

Twenty-four hours later, they take the President of Nigeria on his tour. Hidden in a truck of the official convoy, Maurice is taken along to adjust the brakes again if necessary. He returns home late at night.

Early next morning, Henri and Maurice hoist the engine out of the Deuche and take it apart on a bench. They clean the parts with petrol, prepare the new crankshaft and start reassembling it. Everything goes back together nicely. In the evening, the Franco-Nigerian is surprised to find the new twin-cylinder back in its chassis and in running order. The 2CV has its so-recognizable signature sound back again.

The next day, at seven in the morning, the panicked Franco-Nigerian is banging on the door of the hut:

"Hurry, hurry! The police are coming to arrest you!"

"What's going on?"

"They found out you don't have Nigerian visas."

They grab their belongings, throw them in the car and get in… As they're leaving, Maurice hands the rifle and ammunition to the Franco-Nigerian:

"Here's a gift."

"No, no, I don't want…."

"Yes, take it! It can help you."

A fortnight later, the Aubervilliers trio will hear the news: a coup had just occurred in Nigeria…

12

The big rainy season

In Cameroon, they face a season of biannual torrential rains that descend on the equatorial vegetation belt.

By day, they drive through thunderstorms the like of which they had never seen before; by night, so many flashes spear the darkness that the sky seems to be on fire:

"It's like being pursued by thunder and lightning…"

"It's crashing on all sides, not to mention the gales!"

"It feels like the whole world is furious!"

Alone in the bush in their 2CV, the four Elements—Fire, Air, Water and Earth—seem to be in league and unleashed against them. As if the forces of nature were hurling spears of light from the sky and bombarding their tiny steel ship with terrifying thunder.

At the risk of being soaked, they can't get out or make any food. Insulated by tires, on the principle of a Faraday cage[14], the cab acts as a shield against the lightning. A tumultuous din envelops the solitary progress of the Citroën. Likewise, all the frightened animals, from big to small, hide in the depths of the thick forest. On the narrow-curved track, the Deuche staggers between flooded verges on both sides. The incessant rains have turned the hard-

---

[14] A Faraday cage is a metallic enclosure that prevents the entry or escape of an electromagnetic field. A heavy-duty Faraday cage can protect anyone inside against direct lightning strikes.

packed surface into a slippery mess: Henri can barely keep the car on the road. Suddenly, the Deuche slides sideways into a rut. "Don't you know how to drive!" cries Maurice.

Under an icy deluge, the trio climbs out of the car. The rain pummels them like stair rods with a frequency and force unknown in Europe's continental climate. Their heads drenched by ice water, the three Parisians' teeth are chattering.

The 2CV can't make it out of the ditch under its own power: the two-wheel drive is spinning. The three companions empty the van, take everything off the roof rack and put the suitcases in the mud. Finally, working together, they lift the van and move it bit by bit…

Each time they get bogged down or succumb to the elements, they push like true pioneers and eventually manage to put the 2CV back in the middle of the road. They then load their gear back on, hop into the cramped cab and put on dry clothes. Henri is about to take the wheel when Maurice says, "Move out of the way."

He grabs the steering wheel, gets going and manages to stay on the road for about two miles in the same awful conditions. Then crash! The Deuche slips again… Dismayed, all agree:

"That's enough, we're staying put! At least we're dry…"

"Yes, it's enough for today."

"Kill it for now. Let's see what it's like tomorrow…"

Then they fall asleep, making the most of the lack of comfort in the 2CV. Nodding off, Henri realizes that a single cylinder would really have been insufficient in the rainy season. A good decision has meant a better future…

In general, when they can drive, they drive. It all depends on how tired they are. But some days are exhausting. Especially when they've driven the whole night, because by day the weather is absolutely unsuitable. Moreover, camping is impossible because of the rain.

One rainy day, while navigating with headlights on, with Mauricette and Maurice sleeping on the bench beside him, Henri drives as fast as the width of the road will allow. Suddenly, he spies huge ruts in the distance, where the earth seems completely plowed up. On the left, the terrain looks better.

Turning the wheel slightly, he corrects his line of travel, but skids... On a slippery, muddy slope, the car is sucked in and is heading for the river at full speed. He stands on the brake with all his might, but the car keeps sliding until it finally stops in the middle of the river. A great crash sounds out to scare all denizens of the woods! Henri didn't have the time to see the bridge. Drama inside the 2CV! Startled awake, his two acolytes show their surprise:

"What the hell are you doing!"

"Why are we in the river!"

Coming down a bit, they ask Henri, "How did this happen?"

Henri can't offer them any explanation. He himself doesn't know how he got here. But this is not the time to start jawing, the point is to get out of the sinking vehicle. Mauricette and Maurice have fully woken up. They haven't noticed the water rising. With the ship sinking, the captain tells his two sailors, "If you don't want to get out, feel free to stay! But I'm getting out while I can!"

Henri opens the door and water rushes in, precipitating the escape of the two castaways, now forced to leave the ship... Discussion continues on the bank. From the road, Henri sees that the line he had taken runs parallel to the bridge and leads right into the river. Six or eight feet above it, the bridge overhangs the roof of the Deuche. We'll have to lighten the car as much as we can so we can haul it out with the least damage. But we will wait for daylight, not right now...

At dawn, the three adventurers decide to remove anything of any weight. First, they take out the equipment: the spare wheels, the toolbox, the canteens, the luggage, the tarpaulin... etc. Then, Henri and Maurice go back into the river to remove the hood, the fenders and anything else they can. They put it all on the bridge. It's the only place around here that's out of the mud.

The rain has now stopped.

They cut big pieces of wood, long and solid to use as levers; knowing that no car or truck will be passing by for two or three months... maybe longer. Armed with these big levers, little by little they back up and elevate the Citroën but it's an enormous effort. They block the wheels from moving with rocks and apply the hand brake until the engine emerges. Letting the water drain out, they wait.

Suddenly, a man with a bicycle balanced on his head appears from nowhere… Strange because they hadn't been through a village in a long time.

This "good Samaritan" will help them rescue the 2CV. When he thinks the car is ready to start, Henri puts it in reverse and engages the clutch. Thanks to the long levers positioned under the bumper, Maurice with the stranger's help manage to gain ground inch by inch… They haul the Deuche onto the bank and up to the road.

Mauricette has made coffee for her musclemen. The trio share some with the wilderness stranger, who will leave as he came… his bicycle on his head.

The young woman takes advantage of this break in the journey to do her laundry.

That evening, they load the gear back into the car, cross the bridge, and head optimistically through central Cameroon for Yaoundé…

At the western Cameroon border in Garoua, a customs officer had given them a personal letter for his brother, also a civil servant in the southern Cameroon border post in Ambam. As they head south though Cameroon, the roads become wider: they're in better condition thanks to the logging operations along the route. The 2CV crosses the Pygmy region and arrives in Ambam near the border.

The officer's brother on the southern border welcomes the trio with open arms, happy to receive a letter. In typical fashion, his family offer them their hospitality and share with them food and lodging. That night, Henri and Maurice get to know the local medicine men who, through symbolic and rhythmic dances, introduce them to their ancestral folklore.

During the last meal, the guests are asked about their plans:

"Why don't you stay in Cameroon?"

"We're heading further south, to Gabon…"

"You know, we're always looking for mechanics to service machinery. You'd have a job in this country."

"You could take care of a cocoa plantation: we could offer each of you a concession, if you decided to stay…"

"Thank you, but that will not be possible. We're really determined to go to Gabon."

Kindly, Henri and Maurice decline the offer, but their Cameroon hosts have a hard time understanding this decision.

Although they could have stayed close together and had work in the same organization, but less well paid than in Gabon. For this simple reason, the trio of adventurers did not want to stay. Courteously, they take leave of the customs officer and his clan after their three passports are stamped.

Crossing the neutral zone between the two nations, they take to the road again. Unfortunately, in this border corridor, they drive over a tree stump and smash the rear suspension. The shock absorber rod is broken... Precariously, the 2CV makes it to the Gabon customs post in Bitam, but is unable to go further for now. Maurice offers to go back to the Citroën garage in Yaoundé by bush taxi. Two days go by. Finally, he returns with the parts. Once everything is fixed, the trio cross the border.

Fulfilling their most cherished desires, they enter Gabon.

13

On the Equator

As the 2CV advances towards its Gabonese destiny, a wheel bearing suddenly cracks. Broken down on this busy road, they will nevertheless reach Oyem under their own steam.

The Deuche makes it to a large Christian mission supported by the priesthood of men and women of the European Church: They bring their knowledge, medical help and care. They teach school and play games with African children in the surrounding villages.

The three friends enter the missionary concession. Trying their luck, Henri and Maurice ask if they know where they can find some spare parts for the Citroën… A priest receives them kindly:

"Of course, my brothers! Come…"

He takes them to where some 2CVs lie abandoned, two or three, more or less dismantled.

"Take what you need to fix it," he says.

In this small 2CV cemetery, assisted by Maurice, Henri carefully dismantles two healthy conical bearings, their cages and lock-washers. The next day he mounts the assembly on its hub, adding some recovery grease.

That evening, the three travelers are invited to dine at the fathers' table. During conversation, Henri learns that the European fathers used to go on holiday to the Sainte-Marthe Cure in Pantin, near his parents' home. Without a doubt he must have crossed paths with them as a child frequenting the youth club. He remembers playing games with priests in white robes: football, basketball, dodge ball… He would joyfully listen to their stories of the simple life as African missionaries, their anecdotes and jokes. Through play, in the guise of the little Way of the Cross[15], the fathers used to teach[16] *the life of Christ.* At the end of the day, the children used to have fun watching Charlie Chaplin movies. All the children scattered happily, wanting to come back the next day as soon as possible…

The trio are offered lodgings inside the mission. They're finally having a good night.

When leaving the next day, Henri, Mauricette and Maurice sacrifice some of their French money in gratitude for the meal, the lodging and the bearings; the Fathers are very happy with their gift.

Late that evening,[17] around 5 p.m., they find the track blocked by roadwork. Road crews are building a laterite road to Libreville, as well as one or two bridges over the rivers. A European site supervisor is stopping traffic. Henri waves to him:

"Hello, what's going on?"

"You can't go any further."

"But we're going to Libreville…."

"We're already having trouble getting through with our Land Rovers, so you won't be able to get through with your 2CV!"

"The road is that bad?"

The only response they get is a long silence…

"Alright then, we're going to park by the side of the road, we're tired! Can we camp here?"

"Yes, if you want…."

"And I'll try talking with you in the morning."

---

[15] The Way of the Cross or the Stations of the Cross are a 14-step Catholic devotion that commemorates Jesus Christ's last day on Earth as a man.

[16] In this, they used the pedagogical innovations introduced by Don Bosco in the nineteenth century, and adopted a century later by Robert Baden Powell, founder of scouting, and Maria Montessori, a pioneer in pedagogy.

[17] At the equator, the sun sets at 6 p.m. and rises at 6 a.m., all year round.

"Yeah, maybe things will get better."

Henri maneuvers the 2CV to their improvised campsite, over to one side. Mauricette and Maurice ask, "Why did you say we're tired and are going to set up camp?"

In code word, Henri explains his plan, "Set up tents, eat and rest."

He didn't say that they'd be leaving early the next morning. Around 4 a.m., he wakes up his friends gently:

"Come on, up you get, let's go. Let's pack…"

"Eh, are you crazy?"

"No, I'm not. Can't you see what assholes they are? They'll never let us through!"

"So, what do you want to do?"

"Let raise the barrier, get in the Deuche and go to Libreville. We don't need their permission to hit the road! Let's go!"

The road turns out to be better than anything they've ever encountered before. Keeping a sharp eye out for hazards, Henri puts his foot down and drives as fast as he can. On this future national road, as when off-road, he avoids ruts and takes into account the 2CV's ground clearance. The three friends are experiencing an awesome event in their lives: *they cross the Equator Line*, inaugurating a new life in the southern hemisphere!

That same morning, they arrive at Ndjolé on the bank of the Ogooué. This long, wild river - nearly 600 miles - flows into the Atlantic near the town of Port-Gentil.

Following the meanders of the road to the north, they cross the Equator Line a second time. At 9 a.m., they board the first ferry in Kango, which is the only town offering ferry transportation, and cross the Gabon estuary which gave its name to the Republic of Gabon.

At this point in their trip, the trio has already completed two and a half months of travel!

It is September 7, 1965 when they hear about the passing of Doctor Schweitzer. They hear this sad news on the transistor radio during the short crossing across the estuary to retake the route to Libreville: "Doctor Albert Schweitzer *died three days ago*; he was the founder in 1913 of the hospital village of Lambaréné on the island of Ogooué. This man, known for his *"universal spirit" for being* very respectful of all forms of life, has just died." It was almost as if there was an invisible and unspoken relay handed off to them…

The three friends are nearing the ocean: they feel the iodine and the sea air invading their nostrils. Disembarking on the other bank, the 2CV heads for the Gabonese capital… In the evening, around 4 p.m., they arrive in Libreville, but they quickly realize their predicament:

"Great! But where are we going?"

"We know nothing, nobody…"

The leader of the trio then makes the decision to leave the big city and head away from the capital: "This way, it'll be quieter!"

On the road to the airport, the 2CV passes through a portal as unexpected as it is welcoming. On the pediment, the three travelers read: *Gabon welcomes you.* And each column is decorated with the coat of arms of the Gabonese State, above the motto: *Union, Work, Justice.*

The Deuche hugs the shoreline. The three friends will be able to camp: "This way, we don't bother anyone. And, we have nothing to ask."

On the beach, they clean the 2CV with seawater, remove the dried mud and wash the red dust away. They return the car back to its beautiful black color to look presentable in town.

The very next day, locals are spreading stunning news:

"There are campers on Libreville beach!"

"That can't be true, how did they get there? There's no road!"

Facing the difficulties, thanks to the friendship that unites them, the Aubervilliers trio found among their own resources the help, courage and supportive comfort needed to make the trip.

"When dreams of escape become reality" reads the title of this full-page article in Gabon d'aujourd'hui's newspaper. A young journalist intrigued by this unusual story has just interviewed Henri, Mauricette and Maurice on the subject of their long journey. Here are a few extracts of the press article:

"They passed over mountains and crossed sea and rivers before arriving at their destination in Libreville where they finally got to indulge in a well-deserved rest! On

the beach, early risers of Libreville have recently witnessed an unexpected scenario: campers.

Have the hotels of Libreville been considered insufficient? Is there a housing crisis?

Asking these questions to the three young Europeans as they take down their tent is like entering into the adventure. An adventure consisting of 9,300 miles in a used 2 cv Citroën.

It is in this situation that the trio has been able to overcome numerous problems with remarkable resourcefulness.

The trio is presently residing in Libreville where they've found a place to stay and are looking for employment: as mechanics for the men, and as a waitress for the young woman.

Savings need to be collected before moving on to the next adventure. This might seem like a big expectation for most people, but for them it's not even considered a noteworthy risk. Our adventurous trio is already dreaming of new horizons if the sweetness of the Gabonese way of life doesn't hold them down for good.

A few years ago, the trio would have hesitated in front of dangers and difficulties with advice coming from the imagination of the generations before them who have become imprisoned by their own national horizons. In today's world, exalting dreams of escape are often realized by newer generations who aren't inhibited by the myths and taboos held from earlier times."

14

A New life begins...

Through the kaleidoscope of the countries that they have traversed, the three friends have met people who look different, have different customs, standards, life styles, and skin color. Will our trio fit in? Will they be able to adapt to this new way of life? As a society we have to remember that the freedoms of some, end where the freedoms of others begin...

Our three campers are now folding up their gear and putting it in the Deuche. They head off to Libreville to shop at the Mont Bouët[18] market near an ancient cemetery that had been relocated by a former accomplice of Pierrot le Fou[19] who was himself a very infamous gangster in France. This man having taken refuge in Libreville had two businesses in baking and funeral services and he used his hearse to deliver fresh bread all over the city.

After the shopping in the open-air market, Henri, Mauricette and Maurice see a house in the area with a "For Rent" sign. They rush to the house next door and ask to get more information. The place is immediately available

---

[18] August the 25th 1849, foundation of Libreville by the frenchman Bouët-Wuillaumez.

[19] In the 1940s, in recently liberated Paris, Pierre Loutrel, aka Pierrot le Fou — and his friends of the infamous "Gang des Citroën Tractions Avant" gang consisting of police and criminal members of the former Resistance — was Public Enemy No.1. Loutrel commits burglaries with unheard-of audacity, seduces the most famous stars of the time and has the police running around in circles. See. *La légende de Pierrot le fou.*

for 35,000 CFA francs a month – 70,000 French francs – plus charges. They trio seize the opportunity and sign the lease to rent this place located in a working-class neighborhood in the middle of the city.

That night, they sit down and do the math. Their trip had drained their funds and they've just made a financial commitment. They're distraught to learn that a CFA franc is worth two French francs, which they hadn't realized before they left… Unfortunately, they only have half of what they started out with because it's in CFA francs! They're going to have to do something. The good news is that a normal salary expressed in CFA francs is worth double what the pay would be in France!

Realizing that money is escaping through their fingers, the trio make a decision:

"Whoever first finds work takes it!

"Anything, doesn't matter what….

"We need work!"

By the evening's end, they're happy to go to bed and to have a roof over their heads…

In these African houses, apart from the door, nothing closes. The windows made of braided palm leaves lift up and rest on a stick and latch closed for the night. When our trio wake in the next morning they are dismayed, "Hey! Someone's been here!"

Intruders had cut through the foliage and had got in… Under cover of darkness, in front of the bedrooms they had lit sleep-inducing herbs, allowing the burglars to break into the hut undetected. Our three friends find the kitchen window open and Mauricette's purse lying on the balcony floor. Most of their savings had been in her purse, but fortunately the rest was stored elsewhere. Ignoring foreign currency, the burglars had taken CFA francs and some French notes.

All of this increases the urgency of their situation.

Later that day, Mauricette finds a job waitressing and bartending at Hôtel Louis – just outside the city, near the airport. Henri and Maurice take her to work mornings and pick her up evenings. In turn, Henri hears about a European employer who needs a truck driver — He goes to the address and is immediately hired. Thanks to his military service, Henri has all the driving licenses he needs for everything from motorbikes to large heavy transport vehicles.

Weekdays, he drives a bus in and around the Gabon capital, sometimes all the way to Lambaréné some 148 miles away. He leaves in the morning, does his routes and is back in the evening.

When his boss contracts a beer shipment to deliver to Bitam, he pulls Henri off coaches, puts him behind the wheel of a truck loaded with 25 tons of beer and sets him off down the road. Henri delivers the load to a distant warehouse and brings it back to Libreville loaded with cocoa beans. Each trip takes from dawn to dusk. Whenever he can't set off until afternoon, he sleeps wherever he happens to be: in the bush, on an acquaintance's floor or in a meeting hut...

With the routes he services, over the weeks, Henri brings in a lot more money than other African drivers. Henri's honesty puts him in an embarrassing situation towards his colleagues who hide a large amount of money from the bus revenues for their own benefit. The boss wonders what's happening: Henri has clients; the Africans don't have any. Why such a discrepancy? Without knowing it, Henri had disrupted their comfortable world.

Around this time, Henri's boss was also involved in opening a sports hall with judo, aerobics and fitness classes. When he finds out that Henri was a judo teacher, he tried to use Henri's black belt license[20] to legally launch his club without paying Henri for the privilege. The Parisian refuses the unfair deal.

Soon afterwards, the boss fires Henri as beer driver and hires an African instead. The first trip goes well; the second is catastrophic. The European boss is forced to go pick up the little pieces left of his truck, trailer and load at the bottom of ravines.

Back at the Hotel Louis where Mauricette is working, two men come to the bar and huddle confidentially. Mauricette eavesdrops:

---

[20] Crâne Henri, 73rd French black belt obtained at the Institut National des Sports on 7/ 11/ 1959.

"Where can I find two French mechanics?"

"Don't you know mechanics are very difficult to find here?"

As usual, in the evening, our two companions come to pick up Mauricette. Climbing into the 2CV, she blurts the good news:

"North Gabon Automobile is looking for two mechanics."

"Right now?"

"Right away. Tomorrow morning. Can you make it?"

"Do you know where they are?"

"Right near La Paillote nightclub, Garage Geoffroy."

"Yes, near the popular Surcouf restaurant on Boulevard de Mer."

Without wasting a minute, Henri submits his resignation after a month and a half driving buses…

Around 9 am the next day after taking Mauricette to work, Henri and Maurice arrive at North Gabon Automobiles. They ask to meet the boss and he invites them into his office. Maurice is hired to help build the laterite road to Dolisie in Congo-Brazzaville; and Henri agrees to stand in for Geoffroy who is looking forward to being able to return to France for his holidays.

In addition to the salary, Henri is offered the opportunity of free housing including water and electricity. Henri, Geoffroy and the accountant spend the day together; they establish the transfer of authority, and file signatures with suppliers, bankers and the government. The new rookie garage manager will not deal with circulating cash and he gives his approval for large amounts and all current transactions go through the accountant.

The trio move from the house in the Mont Bouët district to a nicer residential area in west Libreville. They have the boss's spacious European house and the garage to themselves… and two big dogs: a German shepherd and a Groenendael who Henri has to take care of.

Thanks to Mauricette having been at the right place and the right time at the bar, they are able to integrate much easier. The trio is very lucky. As soon as they're settled in, Henri and Maurice ask Mauricette to switch to working at a big nearby restaurant called the Surcouf. She gives her first job a one-week notice before resigning. And now, she can get to her new job on foot.

The three friends help each other out. Weeks pass and Henri takes advantage of the garage facilities to get the Deuche repaired. Both chassis bars have cracks at the driver and passenger end. He gets the staff to strengthen the chassis by welding metal pieces onto them. The three young people are now facing the obligations of their profession and their new responsibilities. On Saturdays, they can relax and head for movie-theaters like everyone else, and Sundays they enjoy a well-deserved rest.

Life in Libreville is very similar to life in France. Now and again, they stroll along the beach. By night, lit by the soft glow of streetlights, the Boulevard de Mer offers a warmly, welcoming and lively atmosphere where a solitary ambler's dreams can mingle with the rhythmic whoosh of incoming waves...

One evening, a young singer from Paris arrives at *La Paillote* to perform the latest hits. When Johnny Halliday starts singing "black is black, no hope there..." he nearly starts a riot among his Gabonese audience... It makes Henri reflect and the young man begins to fill uneasy, "I didn't travel all this way to end up with the same life I had in Paris." While observing all of this, Henri makes plans to leave the city and to go live in the bush as soon as he can...

In order to stay in Gabon, a French citizen has to pay the Gabonese administration the equivalent of a plane ticket from Libreville to Paris. By saving from their pay for a few months, the trio set aside the required amount. One day, staff at the garage blatantly steal their money from a drawer. Henri reports the event to the police who conduct an investigation and find the perpetrators. The thieves say they spent all the money "celebrating like Whites". Since the evidence is conclusive, a court ruling will exempt the trio from paying the fee to stay in Gabon.

Shortly after, Maurice leaves the company of Henri and Mauricette. He now heads a roadbuilding project linking Lambaréné to Ndendé to the Congolese border. The Parisian launches in wholeheartedly with the work crew and construction equipment which include three brand new dump trucks to transport the laterite; a bucket loader to fill trucks; a grader; a tank carrier to haul a bulldozer; one or two compressors and jackhammers.

They live by camping on the road as the months go by. They trace a road about six meters wide along the reliefs to connect the isolated bush villages: Fougamou, Yombi, Mouila, Mbadi… When necessary, the headquarters in Libreville provide the worksite by plane or helicopter… The worksite cope with the challenges of the terrain by building four bridges in Ndendé across the meandering river. Occasionally, they have to cut down trees or work with forest populations to deal with the complicated issue of expropriation. They do their best not to disturb the nearby villages, but if a hut happens to be in the way, they provide mandate issued by the Gabonese Government.

By stroke of chance, Henri hears of a ship from England loaded with a cargo of Land Rovers. Being in charge of routine operations, he quickly realizes that winning this contract could give the garage more than a year's work. The accountant suggests he go to Owendo harbor for the latest scuttlebutt and what's being said on the docks.

Curious by nature, Henri asks him:

"What do I have to do to win this contract? What is our budget for negotiation?"

"To estimate a price, you have to know the total number of vehicles as well as the number damaged during shipping."

"Of course, we can't offer a price without knowing how much work needs to be done…"

"You also have to know how many cars are severely damaged and how many have only minor damage… Those with just paint scratches will come out of the workshop right away and be put up for sale immediately."

All the big garages in Libreville are competing for the Land Rover contract!

By offering an all-in price, Henri find an innovative solution. His top competitors end up setting a different price for every vehicle. Consequentially, by working out a median price the young Frenchman is able to win the contract.

Land Rovers in good condition go back to the Land Rover dealers to be offered for sale all over Gabon and in neighboring countries. Damaged cars are stored separately on a big lot adjacent to the garage.

About 30 Land Rovers are faulty and have been severely damaged during loading or while in the hold…

Since seawater has soaked some of the cargo, there is bodywork damage among the fleet. Some vehicles don't have batteries or spare wheels. Others have bent rims, dented fenders, doors or headlights. There are also cracked windows or windshields which have been hit by hoisting slings...

When ordering replacement parts, the insurer ultimately bears the cost, but the garage has to advance the money and they have to be able to afford major repairs. For every car that comes out of the garage, the garage owner will receive an equal amount. In order to stay profitable, they released five cars a day in working order, repainted, fixed and good to go.

When Geoffroy and his wife return from vacation, they get back to normal daily life. Henri finds it hard to hand back the two dogs who have become rather attached to him, particularly "Mutzig" the German shepherd. The Aubervilliers trio is still living in the guest house.

The next day, around two o'clock in the afternoon, Henri notices: "The garage seems unusually quiet". Seeing the Africans relaxing, he says:

"Hey! My Land Rovers! How are we going to get them out tonight?"

"Don't make a sound, Geoffroy and his wife ask us not to make a noise during their nap..."

The workers were happy to just sit there and do nothing... Henri vents his frustration:

"But they've just come back from holiday, they don't need to be on siesta! Come on, get back to work!"

While discussing this disagreement with his boss, it is the straw that breaks the camel's back:

"Do you want a functioning garage? You have to know what you want..."

"No! We do noisy bodywork in the morning, noon and afternoon I need some quiet time!"

"So fire me..."

15

Test by fire

Forest! Equatorial forest… In Henri's imagination, this is the only virgin place that guarantees freedom.

A typical suburban Parisian, but a bushman at heart.

He feels the vibrant call of the forest. Is it to escape human society? Sort-of… is it to blend in with nature? Perhaps. Is it to feel alive? *Yes!*

Despite his innate ability to adapt, city life doesn't suit him. Some people are sedentary, some are nomads: everyone makes their own choices on how to live life.

The day after getting fired around noon Henri goes to meet a local logger named Mr. Leblanc at a Chinese restaurant in Libreville. As Henri enters the restaurant, he sees Leblanc eating his lunch at a table and he goes over to introduce himself:

"I hear you're looking for a bush mechanic for the logging camps."

"That's right."

"I'm available… and would like to know when I could have a tryout…"

To test his knowledge of welding, mechanics and machinery, the boss immediately suggests a 15-day trial period, because he can't find any European volunteers to work in the bush.

At the Zomo camp between Libreville and Port-Gentil, Leblanc moves him into a big wooden hut with "papeaux" roofing.[21] After about a week, he tells Henri, "For me, it's good. If you want to stay, the place is yours. You can set up however you want."

Since Mauricette has to give notice, she won't be arriving for another week. She settles her affairs and finally vacates her hotel room. As she finishes packing her affairs, the young woman recalls an exquisite moment with Henri while looking for a hotel in Libreville.

They had gone into the lobby and were sitting down in the lounge waiting to check in with a Gabon parrot perched next to the armchairs. Its striking plumage—mostly grey but with a red tail tinged with bright green and blue—said magnificence. As they were admiring the bird, an elegantly dressed African man arrived and strode up to the reception desk. After a lively conversation with the manageress, it was obvious that the man wasn't finding what he was looking for and he turned on his heel to leave. The parrot chirped from the lounge, "Would you like a drink?"

The man turned and replied politely to the manageress, "Yes thanks, if you're offering."

Surprised but somewhat confused, she pulls out a glass and serves him a drink. What else can she do?... but our duo can see she does it grudgingly. As for the African gentleman, he hadn't realized that the random generous offer had come from the multicolored bird. Henri and Mauricette are transfixed by what's happening, struggling not to laugh. While the man was enjoying his juice at the counter, the parrot chirped again, "Do you have any money?"

Thinking this had come from someone in the lounge, the man choked on his drink and turned to cast Henri and Mauricette a dirty look.

When paying for her week at the hotel, still amused by this memory, Mauricette smiles imagining that the manager probably usually says to her husband every evening, "Would you like a drink?... Do you have any money?"

Mauricette checks out of the hotel and takes a taxi to the Léon-Mba international airport. Loaded up with groceries, she enters the terminal where a bush plane stands ready for departure. Henri had asked her to bring

---

[21] Big palm leaves used as roofing.

a week or two of fresh food, which she takes with her on the plane.

After landing, a small four-seater Cessna taxis to Henri's hut and drops Mauricette off at the door. This simple abode will become their home. A week later after finding that they like the camp and have agreed to stay, Leblanc puts the young woman in charge of the camp's minimart which she sets up in a corner of their hut. Now Henri and Mauricette both have responsibilities.

Payday Saturday at the camp starts early in the morning and last until 6 in the evening. At noon, Henri's first big task is to hand out the monthly wages to the workers. Henri is expecting the proper amount of three million CFA Francs to hand out to the workers but is shocked when his boss only gives him one million.

Anticipating trouble, Henri worriedly asks, "What am I going to do?"

He suddenly feels uncomfortable with what's happening.

"What have I got myself into?" he thinks.

Leblanc comes over to the living room and sits next to Henri. Handing over the reins to the store, he reassures him with these few words, "You'll see!"

Henri's having cold sweats over this… but he reassures Mauricette who is unaware of the situation, "Come on, let's get to work! We have to hand out the pay! Don't be afraid to sell to anyone who has money; you sell!"

When Henri runs out of money, the boss abruptly interrupts addressing the workers, "Enough of this now! I need a drink! I'm tired!" He adds, "Buzz off for half an hour. You are not the only one who needs a break. We'll continue after…"

Henri frowns wondering what's going on, Leblanc murmurs, "Go over to the minimart and grab all the cash from Mauricette then come back here and we'll keep going."

Henri rushes to the store and quickly counts the cash in the register. He writes a receipt for 1.2 million CFA francs, puts the notes in an envelope and starts handing out more money with his boss. They continue the same process until 6 pm. Any left over at the end will be used for the store's cash float. Held in suspense all afternoon, Henri now understands why the store was restocked to the brim two weeks ago. If it ran out of stock, the boss wouldn't get his money back and wouldn't be able to pay all the workers.

One month, two months and then three months pass when surprisingly a strike occurs: one Monday morning, while Leblanc is away in Libreville, Henri finds himself alone facing 80 men standing united behind their leaders determined to carry out instructions. Are they testing out the young boss's leadership? In any case, it will be an initiation by trial for the young Frenchman:

"We're on strike!"

"So, you're on strike? Okay, great – me, I haven't even had time for coffee. I'm going back into my house…"

Henri returns to the hut and wakes up Mauricette:

"The men are on strike!"

"So, what do you want me to do about it?"

"Can't you think of something?… anything?"

"No… let me sleep…"

He was hoping for some words of comfort but finds Mauricette half-asleep, seemingly totally disinterested in what's happening. As he sips his coffee, he has an idea. He grabs a piece of paper and a pencil and returns to the garage where the four trucks wait at the beginning of the day to pick up workers. Henri arrives feeling pumped up and addresses the strikers, "Okay, I've had my coffee, now let's talk about work! Everyone who wants to go to work get in the trucks. Anyone who doesn't, give me your name and I'll fire you right now!"

Determined, he approaches an old hand and says authoritatively:

"Your name, or get in the truck."

"Why? You know who I am!"

"No, today I don't know anyone. So give me your name or get in the truck."

Henri watches him pick up his lunchbox, machete, poncho, and climb on board. He goes up to another old man and addresses him the same way, "Your name, or the truck!"

Grumbling, the man picks up his things and gets in the truck. Seeing this, the younger ones pick up their bags and get into the vehicles. And even the drivers follow along. Hearing the engines start up, Henri reckons he's won the standoff. When the driver of the first truck starts pulling out, he shouts, "You're half an hour late leaving. So don't even think about coming back before five thirty. If you do, I'll dock you all a half hour's pay!"

The four Mercedes trucks, loaded with the work crews, take the logging road to work. Not one person had been fired! Ever since then, the camp has been running like clockwork.

If thinks had gone differently, Henri and Mauricette would surely have had to pack their bags and go.

Days go by. Years go by…

After two years in Gabon and now with a small nest egg, Maurice returns to France, leaving his friends behind. Without a doubt, he misses the French way of life.

16

Life experience

In France, when he was a child, Henri had met a Talking Tree for the first time around the age of seven. Not knowing what to do, he hit the Tree with a stick whereupon the Tree said, "WHY DID YOU HIT ME?"; and then more insistently, "WHY DID YOU HIT ME?" Did he hit the tree or *the divine Spirit—his Thought Adjuster*[22]*—*who happened to be inhabiting it at the time?

This mystical experience had troubled him deeply. Fearing that adults wouldn't understand, he kept this experience to himself. But inside, he always wanted to understand it and perhaps meet other witnesses. Consciously or not, rather subconsciously, he has pointed his life in this direction, hence his desire for travel and his attraction to the bush...

In the middle of the Wonga Wongué reserve—pronounced, "Bonga Bongay"—the Zomo camp has one of the most beautiful bush airfields in Gabon.

Flying instructors and their students from Libreville International Airport love landing here. They often have their landings validated by Henri, Mauricette or the owner of the camp. The visitors are often get offered refreshments. It is a great way of adding flying hours to their eventual pilot's certificate: just sign the logbook and leave. Even when stuck in the bush, they all contribute to the country's progress...

---

[22] Cf. THE URANTIA BOOK, Paper 107, Origin and nature of Thought Adjusters.

The landing strip is built and maintained using earth-moving machines including a bulldozer and grader. The laterite sandy runway is nearly a mile long and 40 feet wide with a 15-foot wide cleared shoulder on each side. The 3,500-foot approach has been cleared of trees and takeoffs are gradual with foothills in the distance.

In the afternoon sun, Henri is busy in the garage repairing a logging truck when an elderly worker comes to see him and hurriedly says, "Sir, the plane's finished falling!"

And whenever an airplane lands, Africans say, "The plane has finished falling."

Henri listens but doesn't answer.

"Sir, the plane's finished falling!" he repeats.

"So I've heard," he says, a bit surprised.

The African insists, "But boss, the plane's finished falling!"

With this third time, Henri gets annoyed, "Stop, don't bother me with the plane, I get it!"

At the same time, he suddenly realizes:

"You mean the plane's crashed!?"

"Yes!" says the African, relieved.

Henri reacts and takes matters into his own hands, "Why didn't you say so before, idiot! Don't you speak French! Come on, get in the car, we're going to the airfield... quick!"

Upon arrival, they see a Cessna upside down, two wheels in the air, wings set flat on the ground, they approach and notice that the fuselage is twisted. The plane is wrecked. They then see three military officers, captain, commander and lieutenant, coming out of the French Air Force aircraft, saying, "Everything's okay... We just landed badly."

They were in shock but otherwise uninjured. Henri gets them into the Land Rover and drives them to the hut where Mauricette will take care of them. A little later they will have to find a way to warn the military camp in Libreville, because the plane is a write-off...

The radio is not working.

Henri takes them to the police station in Foulenzem situated 30 miles from the camp where they find a transmitter and contact their base. Another plane will pick up the officers and take them back to Libreville. After dropping off the men, Henri drives back through the labyrinth of forest roads and gets back to Zomo an hour and a half later. Seemingly simple trips like this can actually be quite dangerous and one is never sure of reaching his destination. There's nothing but wildlife along these roads in the bush.

In the bush, the French couple is really isolated. If the situation ever called for it, Mauricette would have to ask a passing logging driver for help: go to Foulenzem, Henri's up there somewhere, you'll find him! At the time, Foulenzem was a thriving logging town of about 2,000 Blacks and about 30 Whites, who made railway ties for the whole of Europe. The specialized wood of this area was a rotproof species called "ironwood". The difficulty with these logs is that they are too dense to float. As a result, the ties are cut in situ at sawmills and shipped by sea.

Back at the Zomo site, where Henri had returned, about 30 men cut mainly Okoumé. Using a dozen chainsaws, they cut the logs of these huge trees which are sliced to make plywood. Oddly enough, the lumberjacks can't make their log quotas.

"The saw's not working!" they say.

Things are always going wrong! Mechanics find sawdust in tanks, damaged spark plugs, torn wires, or a saw crushed by a falling tree. They barely manage to cut 30 trees a day with all hands working. And they are constantly ruining the equipment. Henri and Leblanc have an executive meeting to find a solution and get the loggers back on track. They finally had reached a breaking point and they couldn't keep going on like this. And after brainstorming, they come up with the idea of "freelance loggers". Now, all equipment and resources will be financially managed by the freelance loggers including gas, parts and chainsaws which would be deducted from their next paycheck.

This changes everything.

For example, the boss always used to sell them gasoline. Where else could they get it? Suddenly, 1 gallon of gas per saw is enough instead of the usual 8. The same goes for oil. As for the chains, the freelancers could sharpen them themselves—they just have to buy the files. Now a freelance logger can fell thirty trees a day, the exact amount that can be hauled out in a day. So, one man is enough!

As a precaution, the logging yard keeps two "freelancers" but they need to be slow down because they are paid by tree. They just keep cutting! So, the company adapts and no longer pays for loggers, but instead pay for the labor itself. All they have to pay for now is the mechanical work. Henri and Leblanc have created a win-win situation. Curiously, the saws don't break down anymore which had previously created frequent work stoppages… The freelancers get paid well and the boss wins because he only needs two men instead of eight or ten. There's no shortage of wood and the senior mechanic no longer has to repair saws. All of the sudden, the freelancers know how to maintain their equipment themselves!

That unforgettable day realizing the situation the boss starts feeling very old:

"All my life, they've taken advantage of me! For more than twenty years! I can't believe it! Really…"

"They're stupid, but they aren't as stupid as you think," adds Henri with a smile.

"I never realize," he admits.

In two or three months, the saw is paid for. From now on, the workers are completely independent.

Henri is very happy to get rid of the job of servicing small equipment. He can now concentrate on big machines: loggers, bulldozers and forest tractors… One day, Leblanc asks him to replace the tracks on a bulldozer. Usually, the boss uses a crew of thirty men for the task. He leaves Henri with the bulldozer, the spare parts, the men and an old GMC truck. Henri thinks to himself, "I don't need these thirty layabouts. With a cable and the truck, I can do it myself." For him, knowledge of machinery comes naturally.

So he cuts the old tracks off the bulldozer with a cutting torch: they roll off. He installs new tracks end-to-end and connects them on both sides; then he drives the machine slowly onto them like a train onto its rails. With the truck and a cable, he pulls the track onto the top rollers and slides it along;

placing it on the sprocket wheel he then inserts the pin through the links to lock it. Done! At five that evening, the boss comes back. He's very surprised to see that the tracks are installed. It usually takes him several days with a team of 30 guys to do the same thing. He can't believe it!

The bulldozer is almost finished and ready to go. Since everything's almost finished, the boss calls Henri over:

"You've made them work too hard... you've pushed them too much!"

"Your layabouts? They didn't do anything! I don't need them; they're only pissing me off being here!"

"How is it possible?"

"I just need two men and the truck. Everything else is superfluous."

The only thing left to do is to tighten the two guide wheels, put back the four missing track pads. The bulldozer will be ready to go: "It's back for a turn!"

The employer had always thought that he needed many workers. He now understands and realizes his misconception... at the end of his career. These experiences have been mutually beneficial for both Henri and his boss. "Experience is not what happens to a man; it is what a man does with what happens to him," wrote the British philosopher Aldous Huxley in 1954.

Human experience is the forge of the soul.

17

A village in the bush

Henri and Mauricette share life with the Gabonese people: they live in a hut, occasionally hunt with them, work with them and offer them basic medical services.

Although Henri has great hunting abilities, he isn't a big hunter. If he kills an animal, it's only out of necessity to provide food for the people of the village. The meat of a bush elephant can feed the whole village for a month.

The communal society of Africans stripped of its archaic appearances and clothes of poverty reveals great wealth. In what a busy ethnologist or inattentive stranger considers and ignorantly calls "their culture", you can see hidden in their eyes an expression of original humanity. Suddenly appearing, bright and pure, like a ray of light spearing through a cloudy sky, you can see it if you live daily with Africans and are observant. It's there for you to discover…

The village's child…

In Zomo, life follows the rhythm of the forest. One day, a mother dies in childbirth but the newborn is saved; he is the first child of a young family. Three or four days later, his father dies of a work-related accident. While felling a tree, a branch kicked back, hitting him hard on the head. The newly born child will never know his father or mother.

His first name is John. Since he is very small, the name Little sticks to him and he grows up with it: so "Little John" remains his name for life. One evening, the entire village gathers in their meeting hut and all agree that he will be their communal child: Zomo's child! The little orphan will be clothed, nourished and housed by everyone. The village is his family, everyone's home is his home and he has many brothers and sisters. He's alone in the world, and yet has the biggest family! Raised by all, he will grow up hale and hearty like any child and even end up working for the same logger that his dad had worked for. The worst thing to do would be not to hire Little John... the village's child.

The funeral at Zomo...

On another fateful day, a man dies in the village of Zomo. After some preparations, people decide to bury him the following day. Around nine o'clock, Henri and his men put a makeshift wooden coffin into the Land Rover pick up. Moving barely at walking pace, the hearse takes him on his last journey. The villagers walk behind it in procession; mourning, weeping and crying in inconsolable pain. They all go to the cemetery about a mile from the camp where they arrive near another forest path and they discover a superb antelope. The funeral procession immediately stops and the Africans scatter around shouting.

Henri hears, "Meat! meat! meat!"

Everyone runs to hunt the antelope because they all want their share. Henri is left sitting alone with the corpse in the hearse. Half an hour goes by.

The Africans have killed the animal and divided among them the meat with a machete. They all return with a piece of antelope on the shoulder and immediately resume the ritual weeping, lamenting and wailing.

Henri gets the hearse going again and arrives at the open grave, dug the day before. A few men lower the coffin, bury the deceased and place all his personal belongings on a small mound. Then they all go back to the village. The next day Henri passes by with one of the men from the garage and spontaneously says, "Let's go to the cemetery to see the grave."

When they arrive at the gravesite, he sees everything is gone from the mound; the earth has been turned over and even the corpse has disappeared. Henri's dumfounded. "What the hell happened!" he says.

The African calmly answers, "It's nothing, sir. The spirit's taken everything."

His answer makes Henri angry; he shakes his fist: "That's bullshit! You see this? If I stick this in your face, will you still tell me it's the spirit?"

Henri doesn't like being told yarns.

But with a broad tolerance and strict independence he leaves it at that and turns the page. He ends the discussion, "Come on, get in. Let's go to work."

It's all over now. They were just passing by, just to have a look…

Dog soup…

When Henri and Mauricette had first arrived in Zomo, Leblanc told them this story, well-known among expatriates:

"Be careful with your pet here… I had hired Europeans, a mechanic and his wife, who had brought their small dog with them. One Sunday, invited by friends to a nearby logging camp, the couple goes for a drive. They leave a boy helper, who cooks for them at home, alone with their little dog with brief instructions:

"We won't be home until tonight, so don't forget to make the dog's soup."

"You understand?… we'll be back tonight."

They have a great day and as agreed, they return home in the evening. While the wife is busy setting the table, the husband finds it strange not to see her dog but then thinks nothing more of it. Dinner time arrives and the boy puts the big stewpot on the table. When they lift the lid they discover the boiled dog! They're stupefied!

The cook quickly replies, "You told me to make the dog soup! I made the dog soup!"

After all, the two sound the same: dog's soup and dog soup…

The tame mandrill...

On a sunny Sunday, Henri and Mauricette go to fetch water with the "Scout Car", an American all-terrain vehicle. They approach a small river with the intention of filling five or six 4-gallon jerrycans. Each week, they replenish their supply of filtered water which they use for drinking and cooking; they purify it with a Buron filter and a simple set of interconnected pipes. Meanwhile, their mandrill monkey is on the loose. It's a very recognizable African monkey with its distinctive blue and red snout. The French couple had found it with an injured arm and had taken care of it until it healed. Off it goes, having a little fun in the bush. As they watch it jump from tree to tree, Henri turns to Mauricette:

"How about we'll leave him here and let him go."

"Yes, that's a good idea."

As soon as the water cans are loaded, they get back in the Scout Car and Henri starts the engine. Shrieking, the mandrill rushes to the vehicle, grabs onto the steel cargo hoops and swings into the cab. As if to say, "Daddy, daddy, don't leave me here! Have you lost your mind? What'll happen to me? My home's with you!"

This anecdote shows that primates, called "little brothers" by Africans, have awareness of absence and can feel anxiety; and proves, if proof be needed, that animals have emotional intelligence and feelings.

So why take offence when we say we're all animals in evolution? Aren't they smart? Aren't they capable of communication? Aren't they sensitive? Aren't they loving? Our "little brothers", so to speak, have many things that we can learn from them.

Contrarily in France or in Europe, we no longer live with wild animals. So how do we learn *the Great Secret of life*? How can we know and understand the Universal Love animals give us, that the animal kingdom reveals and transmits to us?

18

The middle way

How can we live more naturally working within the constraints of civilization and escape the materialistic limitations of society?

Aren't there actually two forces, like the *yin* and the *yang*, one passive and the other dynamic? Don't they intertwin in a way that the two together can be found in every individual and society? *Isn't there actually a harmony to discover among all phenomena of life? Aren't they not like the two platforms of a balance scale capable of reconciling opposites?*

Men and women should dwell more often on such thoughts. In France, Henri has a deep feeling of not benefiting from anything. According to him, "Life passes without anything to learn. Nature can tell us nothing because we see nothing of nature: we live almost contrary to nature, against the flow of life."

In the primal forest, Henri and Mauricette are in their element. Mauricette has acclimatized well to this life in the bush; however, she feels the need to sometimes go to the city while Henri doesn't have the same inclination. No problem: she goes there and it doesn't bother Henri.

In the bush, Henri may end up working twice as much, but more freely: what's not done today will be done the next day. He may decide to stop, pick a lemon, orange or grapefruit, and enjoy their juice.

On Sundays, Henri and Mauricette often drive to the beaches. They can trustingly leave the house open and when they came back, nothing's gone.

Try to do the same in France or in your own country and see what happens…

Living in nature makes you feel alive! In the early morning they discover panther footprints right in front of the doorstep… It's a beautiful thing. When one gets up at night one can see animals passing by. Daily life is surrounded by beautiful wildflowers and the cries of all kinds of multicolored birds.

For Henri, there is in the bush a freedom and above all a Love, that can be found nowhere else. In a city, this Universal Love seems absent. In a city, he finds it absurd: he lacks air to breathe, and space. He feels like a prisoner. In a city, he wonders, "Why are there savages who want to dominate me all the time, rob me and assassinate me…"

Naturally, some people are afraid in the forest. Well, let's hope they don't come to live here! Others, like Henri and Mauricette, enjoy this wild environment and find it relaxing.

Imagine when an elephant comes scratching against the walls of the hut; raising his big trunk and letting it fall on the logs is wonderful despite the inconvenience of seeing the hut shaken.

In the forest, everything is camouflage, everything is alive. Everything lives, everything moves, sometimes at the risk of its own life.

One day, as usual, Henri goes down the Ramboué river in a dugout canoe. Suddenly the engine fails: the river takes the skiff with the current and silence overcomes. Henri is amazed to see one then two crocodiles emerging near the slender boat and finally an entire silent crowd of river crocodiles surrounds him. Before this breakdown, he would have sworn to anyone that there were no crocodiles in this river.

On another occasion, the Parisian goes downriver to get a supply of cassava[23] for the village. A sudden wind triggers a set of three or four waves, like a tidal bore. To avoid them, Henri steers to the bank and clings to the mangroves. As soon as he reaches shore, a boa drops from the trees with an enormous splash! Fortunately since the boat is still moving, the boa constrictor doesn't fall into the dugout but into the water.

Animals living in the wild consider nature as their own. From Henri's

---

[23] Cassava is known to be the bread of African people.

experience, if you leave them alone, they won't hurt you! Man however is capable of harming for no reason! Who in their life hasn't heard someone say, "Why did he throw a rock at me, the idiot?" or "Why did he hit me?" Man isn't evil, but learns to be, for he has to defend himself against everything for his own survival and the survival of the people he loves.

Henri reflects in silence and seeks to understand:

"Coming from a civilized country, why can't I live with my brothers who claim to be civilized and why do I get along so well with savages and live among them in the bush?"

In civilized man there is an aftertaste of savagery because he doesn't control anything. For example, those who have no money will remain impoverished; those who suffer misfortune will continue to struggle…

In the wild, Henri realizes that it is the best and the strongest who win; one kills to survive, not for pleasure. Unfortunately, it isn't always the case and here is a story to illustrate:

Every morning while taking the men to work the truck drivers from the Zomo yard meet a particular bush elephant on the track. The men give it bananas for several months until the point where it is almost tamed. But one day an uninformed hunter, soon after landing at the airfield, shoots the elephant of Zomo coming to the convoy for his five or six daily bananas.

In the bush, strange as it may seem, not all behaviors are conducive to the prosperity of life; here are two vivid examples:

Whenever they leave a logging camp, Africans cut down the crops and burn the huts they've built so as to leave nothing left.

What a mentality in man! Henri tried opposing them and this custom. It wasn't easy convincing them![24]

"With no one there, the animals will be able to feed on it!" he says to them.

"No sir, I made it, I burn it. Man leaves and takes everything."

"At least leave what you've planted for future generations."

"No, I planted it, it's for me to benefit from!"

____

[24] For a Gabonese, this custom is based on respect for the balance of nature that has been temporarily modified by human presence.

One day, at another logging camp bordering the Ramboué River, Henri built a fountain to make life better for the men, women and children of the African village. But instead of drawing water from the spring they take it from the fountain's basin where the children have begun bathing and women wash their laundry:

"Don't take the water from the basin, take it from the fountain!"

"Why are you hassling me? It's all coming from the river!"

"It's as good down here as it is up there," they say in their ignorance.

After months of effort – since no one can make them listen to reason – Henri makes the decision to bulldoze the fountain and follows through his decision. He's worried about the possible development and spread of diseases and epidemics. But the whole African village is against him:

"The water's flowing!"

"It's all coming from the river! It's clean."

"The White is bad!" they say, totally misunderstanding.

So, to draw water the Africans will continue to go to the river… at least they are safe. Through this experience, Henri understands that one can't bring too much modernity all at once. It's too much of a change for minds that have been accustomed to other traditions, behaviors and customs for millennia and millennia. Centuries after centuries, generations after generations, evolution must advance little by little…

"Evolution may be slow, but it is unerringly effective."[25]

------

[25] Cf. THE URANTIA BOOK, Paper 86, Early evolution of religion.

19

Living with animals

In the equatorial forest, all human senses have to be alert, danger can lurk anywhere. Constantly vigilant, alert, everyone is responsible for their own survival… and that of others. In this hostile environment, you watch over each other and you use simple means to help each other.

Don't go into the bush if you don't want to be in danger! Big snakes, poisonous snakes, crocodiles await you.

In the bush, small animals are the most dangerous because you can't see them!

If you really want to, armed with your courage, you will meet magnan ants and the notorious sangouillas. Let's leave them to themselves to lurk in the shade of the canopy along with poisonous plants, giant spiders and many other animals…

One day at Zomo's logging site Henri goes to get a spare part from the store in the hut. He opens the lock and enters. The doorway only allows a faint glimmer of light: while searching the shelves, one has to know approximately where the parts are stored to find them. When Henri looks down he sees a group of little mice gathering around his feet, as if distraught. Assembled in a circle, they look like they're seeking protection. He watches them with astonishment. Slowly, he pushes them away with the end of his army boots. They approached him again. Intrigued, he thinks, "That's weird!"

Feeling that something is wrong, the hair rises on the back of his neck and an internal alarm bell rings. "Don't stay here!" he says to himself.

This strange animal behavior signals an imminent danger. Henri quickly grabs the spare part he came for, gets out of the hut and shuts the door. Two or three days later, forgetting this misadventure, he asks an African from the garage, "I need a conical bearing; go and get it for me."

The man nonchalantly goes to the store and shortly after Henri hears him howling, "Ah, sir! Sir!" The African realizes he is alone with a big black snake, terror of the forest. A chill runs up his spine.

Suddenly a big noise sounds out… It's our man, crashing through the foliage and wood wall, collapsing the hut. Running at top speed, Henri's helper screams with all his might, "There's the mamba in there! The mamba wants to eat me!"

In an emergency, all site personnel mobilize. Without further delay, the men decide to search the hut to find and kill this lively animal which is both extremely dangerous and very aggressive.

Can you believe it measures 15 feet long head to tail!

Months pass by. One evening around midnight, moonlight illuminates the sleeping huts; Mauricette gets up and takes a few steps in the big open home. Leaning on a windowsill, she takes a moment to savor the enveloping calm of the night. Suddenly noticing her arms are covered with ants, she starts shouting, "Eh… Henri! Henri! Henri!"

Henri wakes up startled. Mauricette runs frightenedly to him and shows him her arms:

"Look at this…"

"Quick! Get in the shower!"

Immediately, Henri explores the outside of the hut with the flashlight. The light beam sweeps the wall and reveals that it's covered with ants; thousands and thousands of them. He exclaims, "It is difficult to believe but they are all magnans!"

He turns to Mauricette:

"We'll have to go sleep with the neighbors! Or…"

"Do you have another idea? What are we going to do?"

"Pull the bed back because it's touching the wall. Let take four shallow plates and put them under the bed legs and then fill them with kerosene. It needs to be kerosene, water or diesel won't work!"

"I'll get some from the tank."

Mauricette comes back carefully holding a bowl of liquid…

"Slide the plate while I lift the foot of the bed. Did you find the kerosene?"

"Yes, I did… I'll fill up the plates now."

"Let's be careful to fold the sheets and mosquito nets under the mattress to isolate the bed. Don't let anything touch the floor or walls!"

Once or twice a year, magnans clean every corner, nook and cranny of the hut.

This unforgettable night, none of them climb up onto the bed. Outside, in their fenced enclosure, the pet monkeys howl and warn people of danger and cling to the top of a branch to play dead. Meanwhile, the magnans eat the food in their bowls but let the monkeys live only because they had fed them. Organized in a colony, these ants invade everything! Without being noticed, these cohorts can completely cover a body. The magnans then attack their prey and devour it, making it almost mad with pain they bite together the second they give each other the imperceptible signal to attack…

On the same subject, during their long trip to Libreville from Paris, the Aubervilliers trio had carried out an experiment at their own risk but no one got hurt, the three had got out of the car right where bands of magnans were crossing. If they had been injured and moving slowly, they would have had no chance of surviving! These experiences reminded Henri of a true story reported when working with Africans:

"Two men were flying in a light plane. While in flight, the engine sputtered and died but the pilot had time to send a mayday to the control tower giving his approximate position. Soon after, it crashed into the forest and into the treetops. During the crash, the occupants were severely tossed around. As a result, the passenger suffered an open leg fracture while the pilot escaped unharmed. The aircraft didn't reach the ground and was lodged in a tangle of branches and vines. Both men managed to get out of the overturned cabin. They settled on the wings waiting for help because they couldn't get down. Since the injured man's leg was bleeding profusely, the blood dripped drop by drop onto the wing and then onto the ground which attracted the magnans who had invaded the surrounding trees and then the plane. Rescuers discovered what was left of the wounded unfortunate man who had been attacked and devoured. Fortunately, the pilot was rescued."

Back home at the hut, on a Sunday, Henri and Mauricette are walking with Kiki—a white-nosed pet monkey. On the loose, Kiki goes wherever he wants in the forest. He sees fruit on a tree and he's gone! He picks it, eats it and continues swinging from branch to branch.

All of a sudden, his masters hear complaining cries: they see Kiki jump from a tree and run towards them like a rocket. He makes a magnificent leap into Henri's arms from about six feet away. Scared, he huddles up against him. "What's the matter, Kiki?" says Henri.

Henri finds the monkey excited and he manages to calm it down a little. Then, feeling an itching sensation on his chest and hair, he immediately understands the situation and says to Mauricette, "The monkey's covered with sangouillas! Quick! To the water!"

They find a stream to wash Henri and the unfortunate Kiki. The monkey doesn't want to be washed. It hates water, so it screams and screams… they finally get rid of these invisible tiny little red pests.

Henri and Mauricette move with their logging company to a new unexploited portion of the forest named Zogo.

The couple now lives on a peaceful hillside that slopes into the Ramboué River where they use a natural dock to transport wood on the river and prepare log rafts towed to Owendo Harbor. They reside in a small wooden chalet covered with sheet metal and are surrounded by a beautiful flowered garden.

One afternoon, while calmly eating their lunch under the adjoining palm roof, served by an African boy, Henri suddenly sees the young man grab a rag and rush towards him: "Don't move! Don't move, sir!" Henri freezes on the spot! Looking at his plate, he doesn't see anything. A tiny poisonous snake is precariously positioned to drop from the palm roof onto Henri. It's a beautiful specimen with beautiful yellow and green colors, but extremely venomous. Immediately, the boy uses his rag and with a swift and precise blow he throws the deadly snake to the side among the trees.

Life resumes its course, punctuated by work. At the dock, near the logs, an African woman goes alone to do her laundry in the current. Hardly had she started when a crocodile surges to the surface. She calls for help and people came to her rescue and chase away the crocodile which plunges back to the bottom of the river. Fortunately, she had seen him in time… otherwise, he would have grabbed her and dragged her down! Usually when approaching the river, Gabonese women sing and tap the water to communicate along the river and to scare crocodiles away.

Playing tom-toms is an art, a precious language that should be preserved: it is part of *the African soul*. But has it been lost? Unfortunately, it is becoming a lost art among younger generations. Experience has shown that a letter sent by tom-tom travels faster than by post office. From village to village, Africans can relay a message and transmit it over long distances. For instance, no sooner had a doctor named Dr Schweitzer left Lambaréné that he was already expected by name in Oyem.

In the natural environment, primitive ways prove to be much more effective than our so-called modern and technological means…

20

The Father and the Mother for them

Daily life at the logging camp involves various responsibilities: organizing the work, supplying the grocery store, handing out the pay, shipping the production, maintaining and repairing the machines. But that's not all! It is also necessary to the couple to settle disputes, maintain a birth register, prepare funerals and weddings, certify civil status, manage the pharmacy, treat the sick and the wounded… and even care for the animals of the forest.

In Zogo, at the same logging camp, circumstances led Henri to open a quarry from which ballast stone would be hauled for the construction of a future railway: the Transgabonese. After several years working on site, there was a six months break in business and everybody left.

When work is possible again, Henri and Mauricette return to their old cottage. Henri finds the garage he built for equipment still intact. When the former workers return to their site, they are happy to find the vegetation and crops. The new workers also profit from the lemon, tangerine, grapefruit, mango and avocado trees which add to the environment. They use the same settlements they had left behind six months ago. The old village springs out of the land and the Gabonese people readily admit:

"Ah, yes sir! You were right to leave it intact. We are very happy to find a hut and crops."

"*If it can't serve me, it can serve others…*"

From Libreville, the railway construction first reaches Owendo harbor and then proceeds east towards Franceville via stations at Booué and Moanda; bridges and tunnels are also built along the way.

In the seventies, the world's longest single cable car runs 47 miles long and is operated from Bakoumba. This impressive construction is used to transport manganese ore from the Moanda mine to M'Binda in the Congo and is then transported to the harbor of Pointe-Noire. Years later, the Moanda Railway Center will carry uranium and manganese to the Owendo harbor ore ships in the Libreville Estuary.

In Gabon, Zogo is the only ballast supplier for the new railway track. The yard works five to six days a week, from seven in the morning to six in the evening – due to the rapid fall of the sun on the equatorial line. At the dock, there's no longer a need for logging installations as new arrangements are being made to berth the boats. The riverbed is dredged so that barges can float at low tide and the riverbank is consolidated with metal beams. The small harbor can now accommodate the rotation of the barges that will sail to Libreville.

To supply the yard, two huge diesel tanks are installed near the pontoons and a power plant equipped with four large diesel engines coupled to generators provides electricity. While Henri sets up the crushing plant, a manager runs the extraction quarry. Henri's work consists of positioning electrical machines, conveyor belts and build hoppers while raw stone is dumped and stored separately on site. Aggregate is produced to the requested size, sorted by vibrators in different grates, then washed and moved out by several mobile "grasshoppers".[26] Bucket loaders will fill barges at the dock; the mountains of calibrated stones will be sent in barge containers and towed by a seagoing tug.

One Sunday, back at the house which had been chosen by Henri for its distance from the festive life generated by the songs and dances of African nights, Henri receives a surprise visitor. It's a Gabonese man coming from the village where around a hundred workers and their families reside. He's here

---

[26] Mobile conveyor belt, used to load trucks or construction equipment.

to pick up Henri to rescue a sick person and the guy arrives in a Sambron, a small tractor with four cogwheels and a large dump attached to the front:

"Sir, there is a seriously sick man in the village who needs help!"

"Can you take me there in your Sambron?"

"Yes sir, it'll be faster!"

Away they go! A bit later, the driver skids off the road and they're both ejected. The man is injured by the starting handle attached to the chassis and his open thigh is bleeding heavily. Some Africans run up and take him back to Mauricette. He quickly becomes the priority in delivering first aid. But they have no coagulant! Henri dresses the man's upper thigh with a tight bandage but after ten minutes it's soaked with blood. Since it's impossible to place a groin tourniquet, he uses a strap around the thigh to try to close up the wound. Every half hour he loosens it but he quickly realizes the bleeding isn't stopping.

In desperation, he grabs the company's walkie-talkie and calls the Libreville base. They're not answering! No one works on Sundays! In Zogo, there is no chance of rescue here without an access road as they are the only site on the Ramboué River. The only way to reach Zogo is boat or plane. It takes an hour and a half by river and half an hour by plane to reach the site.

Henri sends out a mayday on the radio hoping that it can be picked up and transmitted to Libreville. It's his only realistic option and his patient is losing blood fast: he has to do something! He keeps trying over and over again for what seems like an eternity, "Mayday… Mayday… Mayday… this is Zogo logging yard on the Ramboué… I have a very serious casualty, who will not last the night… I have no way to treat him… please send me a plane or helicopter to evacuate him… alert the Socoba Company headquarters in Libreville… Mayday… Mayday… Mayday…"

Fortunately, an airliner 500 miles away has recently taken off from N'Vingué International Airport near Franceville and picks up the message at cruising height. Henri doesn't know if anyone's hearing him. He would later learn that his mayday was passed on to the control tower, which relayed it by phone to Socoba. The company immediately sent a helicopter to take charge of the casualty and the sick man from the village to get them both to the hospital in Libreville.

A good month later, Henri sees the injured man again when he returns to the yard. The man now has eight stitches leaving white scars on his black skin and he can stand and walk normally.

Situations like this are common in their daily life and feeling the Universal Love they care for the children and parents of the community.

One day, a woman brings her sick child to the young French couple. The poor boy's body is stiff, as if cataleptic. Henri takes him in his arms and tenderly magnetizes him for a moment. Bit by bit, he feels each of the four limbs relax: click…click… When the toddler fully recovers, Henri gives him back to the mother, her face beaming. She would later spread the news of the healing throughout the African village.

On other occasion, Mauricette treats a man bitten by a poisonous snake; she gives him a serum injection and tells him to come back the next morning. So happy to be healed, he dances all night. He's exhausted and can't even go to work the next day.

Through these simple acts of charity, they become father and mother of all these Africans.

To say thank you or happy birthday, they put flowers in a can on your doorstep. As a gift they would give you their last egg.

The Africans now call Henri and Mauricette: *"The father for us, the mother for us."*

When the day finally arrives for the couple to leave the camp for good, the whole village comes out to say goodbye at the plane; and many shed genuine tears…

At this precise moment, Henri doesn't know that he is about to make the discovery of his life. Sometimes great joy can follow even after many moments of sadness. Joy often occurs when one does not expect it.

21

A Talking Tree

Years pass by. Henri is working at a construction site in the hilly region of Franceville[27] otherwise known as "Little France" for its similar landscapes. At this time in his life, he's had the chance to demonstrate not only his mechanical skills but also his compassion and understanding of human nature.

He is now responsible for construction equipment, maintenance and servicing of heavy vehicles. One morning, he's ordered to go fix a truck that has broken down on the road to Libreville. It has been stuck for a week in the forest of bees. This inhospitable forest is teeming with all kinds of flying insects—bees, mason flies, horseflies, etc…

All the Socoba mechanics, in the company that Henri works with, have tried but failed to do anything for this tractor-trailer which hauls a bulldozer and urgently needs to be delivered to Franceville.

Once on site, Henri sees at the back of the double axle semi-trailer an end of one of the two axles has fallen off. Harassed by insect bites, Henri and his team start to unload the bulldozer and then dismantle the two twin wheels on the damaged side of the axle, they also dismantle the brake drum, then use steel cables to secure the hub and shaft to the chassis to raise the axle to keep it from swinging. With the other six twin wheels functioning normally, the

---

[27] Town 470 miles east of Libreville

trailer's now running on three legs!

They mustn't lose any of the 30 or 40 tons of cargo.

With the work completed, and dozer back on the trailer, Henri says:

"Come on. Let's go. We're done here."

"But sir, there are no wheels on this axle… You can't tow it!"

"It'll be fine. The other axles will compensate!"

The team of mechanics and even the driver can't believe it… this is the first time they've ever seen a truck with such a load, working with wheels missing. The crew is able to carefully drive the 90 miles back to the garage.

Months later, Henri is astonished to see his truck in Franceville still running with missing wheels; the company still hasn't replaced the missing parts. And it's still running great! Everyone in the streets of Franceville is now used to seeing it like this! The mechanic realizes there are many ways of doing things; it just takes some common sense!

In Bakoumba, another village near Franceville, Henri has the opportunity to care for a young blind man whose father manages a local African restaurant. The child was born with perfect vision but has developed a disease. His red blood cells are clumping and his doctor diagnoses: "It has concentrated behind his eyeballs and made him completely blind. But it's not life-threatening. There is nothing we can do, he will always be blind…"

Taking pity on the child, Henri tells the young boy, "Come on, I'll try to do something for you."

Every day, Henri patiently magnetizes him. By the end of the second week, he can find his way round a house like a child with regular eyesight. The child can now see you if you are close enough to him. Outside, he can now distinguish blades of grass and flowers. He regains some of his vision and some of his life.

After a hard day's work, while Henri and his men are driving back to Franceville, they stop near a small village on the outskirts. Since everyone had worked hard that day, the boss decides to buy them a small local beer called Regab[28], brewed on the Ogooué. After drinking their beer, they get up

---

[28] Regab is the national beer of Gabon.

to leave and they pass by a meeting hut when they hear an old man speaking with a distinct and audible voice, "Tonight, I am talking about the Talking Tree."

"What did he say?" Henri asks his workers.

"He's just said he was going to tell a story about a Talking Tree."

"Can we attend?"

"Yes, of course."

"Then let's go and listen!"

The men go into the meeting hut with Henri who is the only white man in the whole assembly. They sit near the old man so they can hear what he is saying. He tells a story:

"I was a young bulldozer driver when we drove from Franceville to Akiéni. The road is almost totally straight and before we reached Akiéni, we came across a tree in the middle of the road.

One morning, my bosses ordered me to get rid of this tree, they wanted me to pull it out of the way and to cut it into lumber. I ran into it with my bulldozer to try to knock it down and each time I heard,

"LEAVE ME ALONE!"

I was so shocked by this that I became afraid and ran away leaving my bulldozer behind."

Henri is captivated hearing this because he remembers seeing this tree in the middle of an empty plain when driving to Akiéni. It's the only tree in a large stretch of land and in an area that resembles a sea of sand due to over deforestation.

The old man resumes his tale:

"They go to find other bulldozer drivers but the same thing happens again. The White European boss in charge of the work tells us, "You guys are all useless!" and takes control of the tractor to try to knock the tree down himself and to his astonishment, he hears:

"LEAVE ME ALONE!"

He gives up and decides instead to build a roundabout around the Tree.

People passing through Akiéni invariably say, "They left a tree in the middle of the road! That's weird!"

But these people don't know the story of the Talking Tree. For Africans, at least for the older generations who know this tale, it is a true god who reigns in the middle of the track. They'll never touch the Tree! But what will the new generations do? Perhaps they would cut the Tree up into lumber…

After 23 years in the southern hemisphere, Henri and Mauricette can now consider returning to live in France. Thanks to Henri's forbearance, a great deal of patience born from real understanding, and after a 9,300-mile journey away from their native land, Henri and Mauricette have found what they were really looking for. Now Henri understands the deep meaning of his spiritual quest on the African continent and he cheerfully hums an old tune, then sings the words:

♪ A flower in our hat, a song in our voice, ♫
♫ A joyful and sincere heart, ♪
♪ That's all it takes, for us young boys, ♫
♫ To go to the ends of the Earth. ♪
(Bis)

About the Author

If you particularly enjoyed reading this, I would be grateful if you could post a comment on Amazon that reflects your appreciation of this book.

You can connect with me on:
🌐 https://www.patrickpusey-auteur-voyage.com
📘 https://www.facebook.com/patrick.pusey.790